MW01128417

Other books by

Michael Edward Owens

The Way of Truth Eternal – Book I

Babaji – the Beginning Has No End

Ekere Tere – City of Light

Paramitas – The Gathering of Many Rivers

Guardians of the Gates of Heaven

Spiritual Comfort – Language of the Heart

The Crown of Thorns – The Foundation of the Catholic Church

Messengers of God

THE WAY OF TRUTH

The Sehaji Transcripts -

Volume I

Sri Michael E. Owens

OPEN HEART BOOKS

Copyright © 2011 by Michael Edward Owens

Editorial supervision by Michael Edward Owens
  ~ Cover Design: Brett Marshall
  ~ Editing: Paula Greene, Joyce Hofer, Jo-Ann M. Price, and Percy Walcott
  ~ Mind Diagrams: Victor Cebollero & Paula Greene
  ~ Publishing: Rich Price

All rights reserved. No part of this book may be reproduced by any mechanical, photographic, or electronic process, or in the form of a phonographic recording; nor may it be stored in a retrieval system, transmitted, or otherwise be copied for public or private use—other than for "fair use" as brief quotations embodied in articles and reviews without prior written permission of the author.

Disclaimer: The author of this book does not dispense medical advice or prescribe the use of any techniques as forms of treatment for physical or medical problems without the advice of a physician, either directly or indirectly. The intent of the author is only to offer information of a general nature to help you in your quest for emotional and spiritual well-being. In the event you use any of the information in this book for yourself, which is your constitutional right, the author and the publisher assume no responsibility for your actions.

For more information, visit www.thewayoftruth.org
First Edition: October 2011
ISBN-10:1-4664-1161-9
LCCN: 20119182279

THE WAY OF TRUTH

The Sehaji Transcripts -

Volume I

Sri Michael E. Owens

OPEN HEART BOOKS

~Table of Contents~

<u>*Chapter*</u> <u>*Page*</u>

~ Author's Note ~

The Book of the Beginning (BOB) is the mission statement of The Way of Truth and the Sehaji Transcripts are my written notes for my talks in the United States and abroad.

Look into your heart and you will find me there.

~ *Sri Michael*

~ Editor's Note ~

For your ease of further contemplative study, the spiritual exercises are indented and any words you are to speak are bolded and italicized.

Also, the Angels and Masters' names are listed in the Index by their *first* name, due to popular usage. Additional information on these and other Masters awaits you in Sri Michael's other published works.

We hope these formatting changes enhance your enjoyment of this Volume of *The Sehaji Transcripts*. Blessed Be!

Module One:

2005 Sehaji Transcripts

"Secrets of God Consciousness"

Abuja, Nigeria

March 26-27, 2005

From the Silent Ones to the participants of The Way of Truth:

The Call of the Living Sehaji Master

Your gentle way,
Your soft light
Is the intense love
Of Sugmad's grace.

You shall walk with us.
You shall taste the nectar of Truth.
Yours is a wonder to behold.

Bring your children before us.
We shall bless them.
We shall grant them the Truth.
They shall know of God's love.

Yours is the path of the true heart,
Transparent and forever full.
Sugmad's love is your heart.
Sugmad's wish is carried on your breath.

~Sri Michael

Saturday Evening Session, March 26, 2005

Spiritual Freedom and the African Renaissance

Africa is at the forefront of the change in consciousness, and each of you has been chosen in this most holy mission of the upliftment of Africa and its long-awaited renaissance. Towart Managi has been assisting the work of the Light and Sound in The Way of Truth. The Way of Truth is the new path of the Light and Sound that honors each of you and what you have done for humanity and this Earth.

The Spiritual Master Rumi has asked me to read his short poem of admiration for the African people:

"The Light of the Heart is the beginning,
The sound of the truth is forever.
With the love you shall exist
in the heart of Sugmad forever."

The Sehaji Masters of the Spiritual Seas have cast their eyes upon you and have witnessed the love pouring through your hearts as you toiled year after year without complaint. Sugmad has heard your cries for deliverance and It has decided to start the resurrection of Africa's Golden Era here in Abuja, Nigeria.

The Way of Truth is the direct path of God-Realization. The consciousness of Africa is undergoing a great healing as the Lords of Black Magic are being assigned by Kal Niranjan to work in other areas of the universe. To participate in this purification, keep opening your heart to love and detached goodwill. The Sehaji know of the African people's struggles and know there are some trapped in fear. The hands of the Sehaji are extended to be there for them no matter what their situation. All answers of this truth are found in love, and all actions that come from this truth are acts of love. Be of the selfless heart, and, when transgressed upon, ask yourself in times of distress, "How can I bring more love to this situation? How can I bring a higher aspect of love to this person or incident?"

The selfless heart gives the greatest gift, that of love. Do not look for a return for small acts of kindness; instead know that the love you give will move through Africa upon the wings of The Way of Truth's message of spiritual freedom. When we love in this manner, we are free.

Universal Soul Movement

Thought does not exist in the God worlds. Soul directly intuits and reflects what is being observed, much like a mirror reflects the light of the sun. Seeing and knowing in the God Worlds is Beingness. Universal Soul Movement is the discovery of self as God in expression; it brings out the elements of God in soul and gives one the perspective of seeing through the eyes of God. Soul can collapse space and time by being totally attentive to its travels in the God Worlds. Universal Soul Movement can give the participant the reason for the root cause of illness.

Universal Soul Movement attunes the individual's awareness to divine thought, which is different from human thought. Human thought moves in a line, while reflection in Universal Soul Movement expands like a pebble dropping into the water of a clear pond. Reflection expands in 360-degree concentric circles, seeing all points of reference from the center of creativity at one time. Universal Soul Movement transcends the illusion of life; it gives true insight into our family, friends, personal life, and work. Universal Soul Movement moves beyond blind faith and intellectualism.

Other paths of the Light and Sound had problems in getting the seeker beyond the Seventh Plane of existence for the following reason: Followers of these other paths were being kept in the same initiations for fifteen to twenty years. I will have more to say on Universal Soul Movement throughout the entirety of this seminar.

My Training for Mastership

I was trained and initially tutored in my early years under the meticulous eyes of the Tibetan Master, Rebazar Tarzs, and the Chinese Master, Lai Tsi. It was their responsibility to take me through the schools of Transcendental Meditation, Raja Yoga, Kriya Yoga, and Kundalini Yoga. I read twenty or more versions of the Bible and studied out of body with St. Aquinas, St. Augustine, St. John of the Cross and St. Francis of Assisi. I was later taken by my tutors to study under Parmenides, Plato, and Aristotle. It was the great Greek philosopher, Parmenides, who gave us the present name of our mystery school, "The Way of Truth."

I joined the Light and Sound teachings after Jesus introduced me to the Spiritual Master who was written about in the book *In My Soul, I Am Free, by Brad Steiger*. This meeting was one of the most memorable days of my life and was also one of my first Universal Soul Movement adventures in the Inner Worlds. The second phase of my spiritual training began in 1999 when I was approached by the Spiritual Master of old, Milati. He treated me like a son and worked with me, taking me on Universal Soul Movement travels to meet with members of the White Brotherhood and Kal Niranjan. Midway though this phase of my training, Milati introduced me to my two other mentors, Agnotti and Kadmon. These three Spiritual Masters introduced me to more than 300 Masters in this universe and were the next to consult with me over my mission, their areas of spiritual expertise, and to discuss their concerns with their respective students. Milarepa and the Grand Council did not want me to have any significant contact with anyone outside of their choosing. I was placed in a vow of silence until I was approached by Jesus at an event in a spiritual retreat for the Masters on the Ninth Plane. Jesus asked me to write his gospel, which he wanted to be called in book form, *Voices from Ancient Bethlehem*. It is a dialogue with Jesus, his Twelve Disciples, Paul of Tarsus and his Apostolic Community, Mother Mary and Mary Magdalene.

My final stage of training was under Milarepa and his teacher, Marpa, the Head of the Council of Silent Ones. I was taken to the Valley of Tirmir in June 2003 at the insistent pleas of Rebazar Tarzs to receive the Rod of Power. I was told by him to immediately begin rectifying the universal imbalances. Milarepa placed the mantle upon my shoulders with full consent of Sugmad, the Grand Council, and the Silent Nine. No Living Master has the right to pick their successor and choose the time of transfer of their mantle. To do otherwise opens the door to spiritual despotism and abuse of power. The conferring of the Rod of Power is always at the discretion of the Grand Council.

My mission started immediately due to the level of world suffering in Africa, South America, and Asia. The Way of Truth, the new path of the Light and Sound, is not built upon the fancies of mortar and stone, but is built in the hearts and minds of those who follow the Voice of Sugmad, inviting each person to reach within themselves to return home to the God Worlds. I began working with Sri Tindor Saki on the maintenance and regulation of spiritual vortices on the Earth's surface and in the Earth's orbit. An immediate priority of the Grand Council was to insure the completion of the spiritual city of Ekere Tere, the city of pure Light and

Sound. It is located in the high Astral Plane, above Abuja, Nigeria's heart. Ekere Tere is the sister city of Agam Des and is constructed to assist the spiritual travelers of this Earth to complete Best-Laid Plans of the Sehaji.

Over thousands of years, Africa has been the host continent of many great and wondrous civilizations. Its time has returned in this new millennium. Its renaissance has returned like the cycles of all historical processes, and what comes with it is spiritual freedom. The Grand Council chose to start the beginnings of this process in the heart of Abuja, Nigeria because of the hard work the African participants of The Way of Truth have accomplished thus far.

Future Literary Works

Jesus approached me to write *Voices from Ancient Bethlehem*; Mohammed has approached me to write *Mohammed, Man of God, Brother of Jesus*; Buddha has approached me to write *God's Middle Way*; St. John of the Cross and St. Bernard of Clairaux requested the writing of *The Angel Gabriel and the Grail and the Templar Knights*; Krishna has requested the writing of *Upliftment is in Your Heart*; and Babaji has requested the writing called *The Beginning Has No End*.

All roads lead to the Light and Sound, and The Way of Truth leads to all ways of life. The Way of Truth recognizes the sanctity of all faiths, theologies, and life paths. It is the mission of the Living Sehaji Master, Sri Michael Owens, to awaken the essence of the Light and Sound in every faith.

The Way of Truth is constructing bridges of peace and understanding throughout the universe.

How the Spiritual Renaissance Begins

The injection of Sugmad's love for all life will flow in your surrounding area causing a current of love throughout all of Africa. There will come in time a new freedom even within the spiritual worlds, and this alone will have a domino effect upon the spirituality of African people. Much change will occur as a result. Peaceful actions and policies will be implemented by world hierarchies, giving more power and freedom to every individual on this Earth. Discrimination and witchcraft will hide their ugly heads, and Kal Niranjan has agreed to work with us in fulfilling these Best-Laid Plans. The African Renaissance begins here today, as I stand before you. Rebirth begins now, and I have released the inflow and outflow of Love and Truth.

The Way of Truth is all of what other paths of the Light and Sound were, are, and will be, but we will go further into the God Worlds than others. Through The Way of Truth's interfaith initiative our new spiritual exercises and techniques will eventually be made available to all faiths.

For each initiation, the participant will receive a spiritual manual on how to retrieve their initiatory word when the spiritual charge runs down. The manual will also supply mantras to contact the various Masters and wisdom temples on each plane. It is a resource to unveil the Soul Contract of the initiate as well as to convey knowledge specific to the family, personal life and work life of the God seeker. The spiritual manuals for each initiation are slated for completion in the near future.

It is my commitment to get all the participants into a proficient level of Universal Soul Movement and eventually fully established in the God Worlds. In the initiation of the God Worlds, the mental consciousness cannot be used. Soul must be transformed from the singular perspective of the "I" and ego to the consciousness of universal selfhood. Soul in its highest proficiency acts "in the interests of all concerned." To be in God Consciousness, you must ask yourself, moment by moment, "How can I act and speak from the highest aspect of love?" Apply this postulate to every person and event in your life, and you will see over the horizon and directly experience God-Realization.

The participant must move their shifting of attention from Soul Awareness to God Awareness, and this means your consciousness must relinquish all vestiges of self-reference. The God seeker must have his principle beingness be universal in reflection and action. All of you have been chosen to be a part of this universal plan conceived by the Sehaji, Masters of the Spiritual Seas. The Way of Truth is rebuilding the House of Our Father, Sugmad, and this must be done Its way, which is The Way of Truth. To be a Master of your own destiny, you must put aside ego. It is not a necessary tool in the God Worlds. These worlds are unfamiliar to the human mind; the mind thinks, the soul reflects. The mastership awaiting you will enable further balancing of this universe with the fire of Sugmad's love.

How Creation Began

When Sugmad came into the universal void It was alone in the emptiness of space. Time did not exist yet. It knew not what to do at first; It stood motionless as a Universal Soul Incarnate. Sugmad began to reflect and felt a strong stirring within Itself. It began to realize that It did not have to be by Itself. It further reflected and realized that It could not stand in front of a mirror to see Itself, so It projected infinite reductive units of Itself into the void and universal creation began. The Sehaji watched in observance of Sugmad's creativity and appointed Spiritual Masters from outside Its universe to take the roles of Kal Niranjan, the Lords of Karma and Time, and Spiritual Masters to sit on councils above and below the Great Divide of creation.

You as the participant of The Way of Truth will reach the Eighth Plane and will experience the aloneness Sugmad felt in entering the universal void. You must have this experience to embrace your own Godhood. You must know what it is to be at the center of your own creativity. When you stand in the center, you only see what you create. This is the beginning of you as soul being a "Universal Law unto yourself." In the God state, soul's creativity is derived from the universal love for all life.

Africa's Inheritance

From the pyramids of Egypt that stretch against the hot desert sands, I am always with you. From the majestic beauty of the Ivory Coast, Mauritania, Ghana, Cameroon, and Togo, I am always with you. To the plains of South Africa, to the mountains of Kilimanjaro, I am always with you. From the shores of Tripoli to the River Congo, I am always with you. You have the Sehaji amongst you – Africa, open your heart to Sugmad's Love! Claim your spiritual inheritance and take the spiritual mantra, "Gombaya," which means "Africa, how I love thee," into your daily life. Africa, let us be free, let us be free!

A short poem of dedication from the Grand Council to Africa:

Africa, How I Love Thee

My Africa,
I hear your pleas for freedom,
I hear your search for joy.

You are my long felt happiness,
Every girl and boy.

Lift up your eyes, my Africa,
I will make you free.

Be well, my Africa,
I do hear your plea.

Turn your hearts,
To the Light and Sound.
Be steadfast, my Dear Ones,
Do turn not around.

The Light Giver comes to your shores
With joy and love.
The Light Giver brings to you
The wisdom from above.

Do not despair, my child,
Freedom is almost nigh,
God in His infinite wisdom,
Brings the Sehaji here.

Saturday ended with the Darshan from the Living Sehaji Master.

Sunday Morning Session, March 27, 2005

The Spiritual Master of olden days, Nairopa, gives you his greetings and gratitude for the work you do and has decided to release his Eightfold Path to God-Realization to you this day. It has not been available to the students of the Light and Sound since the crucifixion of Jesus under the tutelage of Zadok. I will read to you its contents:

The Eightfold Path by Nairopa

I am here to teach you the Eightfold Path. Many have understood it to be the Sixfold Path, and this is how I have taught it, but there are actually eight dimensions, and I will tell them now for the first time.

1. Love God with all your heart and soul. This must be extremely intentional.

2. Love your fellow humans with pure joy. Allow yourself to see no evil in her/him.

3. Rid yourself of evil thoughts or thoughts, which diminish or reduce others to less than Godly proportions.

4. Eat your food thoughtfully and carefully. (Small quantities are sufficient. Do not overeat.)

5. Consume nothing that has its own consciousness. If you do, then its consciousness will meld into yours and interfere, most likely with steps 1-4.

6. Think of nothing but how you will serve others as God. (This will include your contemplations and meditations.)

7. Know that you as Soul are eternal, immortal, and ultimately indestructible.

8. See your body as nothing but a physical shell, but God's own temple, nevertheless.

This above is the Eightfold Path. Blessed Be.

The Vision of the Grand Council

The Grand Council is leading each of you to be in the God state of consciousness. Spiritual illumination means others will see your heart as the center of your being, and your eyes will be seen as God seeing through you. The mountain's summit is not a rest stop. Sugmad wants each of you to come down from the mountain and share the living waters of Spirit. Be consumed with the eternal fire of love and non-power, which is the high ground of this way's teachings. Everyone here is being trained in their dream states by the teachers of Ekere Tere, whether they are conscious of it or not. Be active in your God Awareness and declare daily your home, job, and family as "Holy Ground" by saying this declaration at the door of your home and workplace: *"Let no thing, thought, nor being, cross the bounds of my home, job, and family, unless it is in accordance with the highest laws of Sugmad."* Then sing "**HU**" three times and begin your day. I do this exercise at my door every day. It keeps spiritual squatters and intruders from accosting your spiritual environment.

Non-power

To operate within non-power means being neither for nor against the daily arguments of life. It works from the balanced act of love. Find the place of love in areas of trouble, and you have found non-power. Non-power is our service to humanity without attachment. The Way of Truth is the neutral way, and it gives credence to the holy messages of all the saviors of this world, from Abraham, Jesus, and Zoroaster, to Babaji, Yogananda, and Kirpal Singh. Nothing can exist without the Light and Sound; religions are dependent on its foundation. We are a Mystery School totally devoted to keeping the essence of the Light and Sound vibrant in all aspects of life.

A Message from Sri Treylen, Guardian of Ekere Tere

Spiritual participants have been active in spiritual classes in the City of Pure Light. The Spiritual Masters tutoring within its gates will be taking students in small numbers at first to make the necessary vibratory adjustments to the knowledge they will be sharing at this juncture of instruction.

Sri Treylen said to try this exercise:

1. See Dan Rin in your Middle Eye, touching the deepest part of your soul.

2. Focus on your Third Eye and say *"TOLA-TU-HU"* three times and allow your consciousness to flow with what is given.

3. The gates of Ekere Tere will open and the Sehaji Order will be waiting for those of you chosen to walk the streets of the city and be taken to the classes being held by the various Masters. There does not have to be a conscious connection to the entry of its gates. Some of you will have an energetic tie with the city and will have a conveyance of knowledge funneled directly into your Soul Consciousness.

4. Do not look for results; just allow quietude to enter into your contemplation. Just Be.

5. End the exercise with, *"Blessed Be."*

Spiritual Master Kadmon in Ekere Tere

Kadmon will work with you concerning your Soul Contract and past karma and will offer methods to improve your life. Your Soul Contract is the agreement you have made with the Lords of Karma. It is the agreement that guides your family situation, your monetary circumstances, jobs, and career. This contract can be completely or partially changed under various circumstances unique to every participant of The Way of Truth.

Kadmon offers a technique to give the participant true insight into the nature of their relationships in love and at work. When meeting a person for the first time, use this contemplation before any intimation and in-depth discourse begins:

1. Go into contemplation and sing the name of the Inner Master, Dan Rin, five times. Then visualize the face of the person in your Middle Eye.

2. Ask them if they are there in your life to collect a debt, pay a debt, or to give you mutual love and support.

3. If they are there to collect or pay off a debt, there will be a degree of pain and discomfort assigned to your relationship with these categories of souls. It is best to send these souls on their way by giving them your detached goodwill.

4. Once the first two categories of souls are identified, ask the Inner Master for the grace of having the karma connected with these people resolved and release you from having to continue a relationship with them. Go into contemplation, visualize their face in your Middle Eye, and thereafter see the Blue Light of Spirit around them. Tell them the debt is resolved, to go their own

way in detached goodwill. Once this contemplation is done, do not resume any further contact with this person. If you do, the Lords of Karma will presume you need the lesson with this person.

5. End the exercise with, "*Blessed Be.*"

This exercise can be used regarding people of all ways of life and life pursuits. You must trust what you receive and move onward with your life, not looking back.

Master Lai Tsi in Ekere Tere

Lai Tsi will be working with participants in the area of thought projection. He will be there providing training on how to give an impenetrable wall of love while the black magician is attempting to manipulate the person's thoughts and thinking processes. He will also train the person how to send back the demonic force being propelled at them. It will not matter if you do not know the magician. Lai Tsi's training will teach you how to detect the work of black magic behind the scenes of visibility. Time and distance will not be a factor in the technique's effectiveness.

Master Agnotti in Ekere Tere

Agnotti will be working with members of other paths of the Light and Sound who have been kept in their Outer initiations for 10 to 15 years or more. Many of these God seekers have been suffering for no reason at all. He will help

Dan Rin in relieving them of their discomfort, be it physical, family, and/or financial. Once they connect and commit themselves to The Way of Truth, then Agnotti and I will start working with them. Sri Agnotti sends his love, devotion, and gratitude to you for your vigilance to The Way of Truth.

The Way to Higher Realms

The path to God-Realization will always be reliant on how our heart is open to the truth of Higher Realms. Letting go of the spiritual luggage will be needed to get to the Eighth Plane and above, and will depend on how we use the faculty of our heart in moving from one state of consciousness to another. The heart has its own consciousness, and its voice is much softer than that of the Mental Body and mind consciousness. In the higher planes, the participant of The Way of Truth must listen carefully to the voice of the heart and bring a discipline of control over the mind and body. All aspects of the seeker must be used to prepare soul for the journey back to God. Whatever divine love is, it is found within the daily workings of our heart and its consciousness.

Many beings from other worlds have come to Earth to observe humanity and the way its heart directs the human will and consciousness. We have not reached the full capacity of using our human bodies and minds. Scientists are still conducting research on the way our minds work and the shape and manner in which our DNA affects the evolution of our intellect and consciousness. The key to the answers these scientists seek points ultimately to the consciousness of the heart. Develop what is in your heart and you will discover divine Truth. The gift of love and its expression was implanted in the heart. This was the way Sugmad gave this gift to us.

The Evolution of Humanity

Mankind's history and evolution has and will be affected by beings who look much different from us, and they will be from distant places. They will still have a soul and also a heart consciousness. Some of the civilizations I speak of will come to us to show them how to express love and develop their heart consciousness. Most of the beings have an over-developed Mental Body, an impoverished heart consciousness, and a neglected Astral and Causal Body. Some beings will be extremely fragile in physical body, and some will come to replenish their genetic pool. What I am speaking of has already happened, will happen again, and will have a significant effect on our mental consciousness, genetic make-up, and physical appearance in the next 8,000 years. I have already seen this on the Earth's time-track and have discussed these matters at hand with the Spiritual Masters of the future. Further details on humanity's interaction with other life forms will be elaborated on in the upcoming book, *Revelations*. This book is an interpretation of Jesus' disciple, John, who spoke with the Seer of Patmos about humanity's last age.

Armageddon is not the end of the world; it is a critical turning point in humanity's genetic pool and world consciousness. John spoke with me about the offering of this book to humanity in one of my Universal Soul Movement experiences. Mankind's survival will be reliant on our use of our heart as a perceptual filter for the raw power of love, along with the effort we make to understand the hidden frequencies and harmonics attached to the energy of the heart consciousness.

Develop the heart and you will attain God-Realization. To delve deeper into the secrets I speak of, study Discourse I of The Way of Truth discourse series. To give you a sampling as to the power of the heart consciousness, I have written down a technique I use on a daily basis called the Heart Technique.

The Heart Technique

1. In contemplation or in face-to-face conversation, envision the heart of the person you are speaking with as a flower. See this flower open and flowing with a golden and blue light of love connecting their heart to you.

2. Let the person speak whatever is on their mind and heart to you. Sing "**HU**" inwardly three times and say to them inwardly, "*In the name of Sugmad, I am connected to you in love and light.*"

3. Allow the conversation to continue and return to singing *"HU"* inwardly as they speak to you.

4. Once the conversation is over, inwardly close the energy by saying *"May the Blessings Be."* Do not look for any desired results in the use of this technique.

This technique is simple but yields amazing revelations in your communications with others.

Past Civilizations

The children of Africa have a special purpose in the Best-Laid Plans of the Grand Council, and this perspective has been on their plate of examination for eons. Africa has been a spiritual vortex of great wisdom for Sugmad, also known as God. It has been foretold that Africa shall once again bring direction and light to the world.

The civilizations of Lemuria and Atlantis could have been saved if their rulers had heeded the spiritual warning given by those seers of the Light and Sound. Many savants of the African continent traveled to Atlantis to warn the peoples of the atrocities they were committing upon humanity and the genetic experimentation in their sciences. This mis-balancing of the Light and Sound reverberated into the Higher Realms. The Grand Council gave Kal Niranjan and the Lords of Karma the right to destroy these two civilizations because of the instability they were creating above and below the Great Divide of reality. The Lords of Karma shifted the continental plates of these two civilizations to safeguard the secrets of their sciences from those who would pervert the Earth again. The closed hearts of these two civilizations sealed their fate, and Kal's dark angels have thus far prevented any human beings from gaining access to the science developed by Atlantis and Lemuria in the Inner worlds.

Of Things to Come

There is a similar imbalance occurring on the Earth again, causing enormous reactions in Sugmad's universe. The imbalance has been festering in the Middle East and Africa due to the level of black magic prevalent in its spiritual fabric. Nigeria has been chosen as the forefront of Africa's renaissance and rebirth. The Grand Council directed the construction of Ekere Tere over Abuja, Nigeria to bring the long-needed order back to the universe. Africa again is the beacon of love, light, and upliftment to the world. There will be a searing truth of such immensity throughout all of Africa that it will sweep through the hearts and minds of all people of this Earth. It will be an irresistible force that will continue to draw souls back to the Oneness in Sugmad's Heart. All of the Spiritual Masters of the past, present and future have been aligning many souls for this time as the great change and awakening starts here and now. It is the end of those dark souls affecting the Earth with their black magic. The gathering of the forces of Light and Sound is a catalyst by which Sugmad's Love will awaken the spiritual mastership in each one of you in The Way of Truth. The waiting is over, and Africa's long-suffering has been heard by the heavens above. Once again, the gleaming spiritual cities and temples will be easily seen and experienced by all those who open themselves to this great wave of love pouring through Ekere Tere above Abuja.

Master Milarepa and the Grand Council Speak

The God power is a powerful tool. Seeking the heart as the center for God-Realization is the beginning of our spiritual journey. The heart reaches out and connects to soul as the way to access all God's perfect and life-enriching eternal sources. The Physical Body is a receptor, the grounding plate for the God power to use in the Physical World. What the heart is for the Physical Bodies, the soul is for the pulse of the Etheric Bodies. One cannot exist without the other. The soul is the perceptual filter for the God power. Soul's development guides the flow, direction, and frequency of the God energy. The soul is the conduit and golden connecting thread that links us to God, also known as Sugmad.

The heart receives Sugmad's shining and illuminating message for a more balanced and thoughtful participation in life on Earth. We are all participants on the road to a more unified planet. Each individual person on this Earth has a responsibility to make our home, this planet, a better place to live. Becoming God-Realized is serving God, and serving God is serving the Earth, from the miniscule acts of giving, to that of the universal. This creates a ripple effect through the far reaches of this universe to the next. The giving of one's self in any form - from a word of encouragement, to lending a helping hand to those in need, to sharing a piece of bread with a child - releases love in abundance. The giving of love opens our hearts to receive more of the Light and Sound of God. Thus it will allow us to become richer in Spirit and abundance on this Earth.

This will translate into better health, prosperity, spiritual gifts, personal talents and skills, and doors will open for new and better opportunities. Give from your heart, not from your hand, and God will give you realizations beyond your imagination. Transformation is a process; it is not an overnight manifestation.

Pay close attention to your dreams. You will have many Masters working with you in your dream state. Journaling your dreams will help you to see with your spiritual eyes the true progress you are making. Dreams can warn you of peril awaiting loved ones or yourself, and/or events of discomfort coming into manifestation. They will help you to prevent what is not a necessary part of your Soul Contract. Dreams can open you to what gifts God has given you. Doing the spiritual exercises daily, studying the discourses, and speaking to your higher self are tools for you to learn how to link to and maintain the flow of God energy from your Heart Center to the Soul Center to God. This connection will experience reciprocal processing through soul as you develop your Heart Consciousness.

The renewing of the God state will occur on a daily basis. This first wave of Sugmad's love will be changing your spiritual signature and physiological composition. This wave will change the face of Africa. The participants of The Way of Truth will be an integral part of this world change. Your Bodies are being used as ground switches for the spiritual vortices being constructed for this wave of renewal. In years to come, you will see positive and uplifting policies in healthcare, world hierarchies, and higher regard to race, creed, and religion. The God-Realized energies will flow through each of you and will penetrate our surroundings, inducing a more powerful love and freedom to all with whom we will come into contact. In the next thirty years, there will be a rebirth and renaissance of the African unity of consciousness and Africa will become a center of intellectual and industrial resources for this Earth. You will see more agriculture, better education for all, and more opportunity to share medical resources and research. Sugmad's love will usher in the Light and Sound to open the heart to greater understanding and goodwill.

The Heart of Africa resides within you, and its pulse resounds with the wind against the trees and flows with this continent's great waterways and rivers. This movement is God's work in progress. Toil the fields of humanity, and till the soil of human communication with love and with the patience of the good farmer. Perform the works of Spirit with love and feel the rush of God's Light and Sound penetrate your very being. Be patient with all life. Things will come to you in the appropriate time. God-Realization and world transformation awaits us all. We are on the path to new freedom within. I would like to end this seminar with a short poem dedicated to the African participants for their vigilant service to the Light and Sound of God:

Walk the Spiritual High Ground

You walk in the dark of night,
You walk in the blazing sun of day.
My heart fills with joy
As you find the Way.

You seek the essence of truth,
The joy that it brings.
You are the center of God,
And carry the truth that rings.

Your heart must open
And give Light to all.
From it love does pour
To answer the call.

Live in the healing rays
Of the healing Light and Sound,
Brought by the Universal Healer,
Who walks the spiritual high ground.

~Sri Michael

"Secrets of God Consciousness"

Oakland, California Retreat

May 14-15, 2005

Climbing the Summit to God Consciousness

The grounding conduit for the God power is the heart, which has its own consciousness; its voice is much softer than that of the Mental Body. In the Higher Planes, the God seeker of The Way of Truth must listen carefully to the voice of the heart and bring a discipline of control over the mind and body. What the mind is for the soul, the heart is for God Consciousness in us. I have spoken with Living Masters of the future and they have related their heartfelt appreciation for the commitment we have made thus far for The Way of Truth. The reflective waters of creativity we are now immersed in are filled with the contingencies of Free Will that have been fully examined in the far distant future. The Sehaji of the present and future have been in continuous interaction with one another. The Sehaji is the wind against the sails of The Way of Truth into the hearts of every culture in the universe. It is my goal to have every participant in God Consciousness. This is the consciousness that must be maintained after the realization of God is attained. Below is a contemplation that will give the seeker a glimpse of God Consciousness.

The Tumultuous Ocean Cleansing Technique

This technique is for those who are working on their God-Realization and are stuck by their own impurity.

1. Imagine yourself in the Higher Worlds of Sugmad. Ahead of you are the falls of the Big Gold River. This river runs tumultuously among rocks and falls several miles below – it is like a big torrent. Above the river is a red sun just like what astronauts call "a big red."

2. Imagine that you are getting into the river where the falls start. You are the same substance with that river; you melt into it and yet maintain awareness of your own self as you now cascade over the falls. It bounces you back and forth, side to side, and all fears and impurity are washed out of you. The falling is to overcome your fears – it is a *sine qua non* (essential) condition to get into the superior part of the Higher Worlds.

3. You leave the river and fly to the big, red sun and enter its heart; it welcomes you with such warmth that you turn pure gold. This is Sugmad accepting you now as the return of one of Its children; this will open

the door for you to know more about God Consciousness.

4. End the exercise with, *"Blessed Be."*

God Consciousness is that state of being where the individual's heart is merged into Sugmad's Heart. This type of heart connection is pure love truly experienced and an ecstatic connection with the Breath of Sugmad, hearing Its heartbeat and experiencing a knowingness of Its universal fabric. God Consciousness, once fully merged, replaces the consciousness of self, and you are no longer the same person. You have been intoxicated by the total bliss of God Consciousness and the only thing that resides in your heart is service to all Its brothers and sisters. The feeling of universality becomes personified in you. In this state, there is a direct knowingness and beingness with everything you come into contact with. The God power in raw form harnesses itself within the center of all your physical and contemplative activities. The mind and ego are placed in balance thereafter and assigned to other tasks in the proper way. The mind works on examples and direct experience. The Way of Truth will build and expand from our example and compassion for the former path and other ways of life. With Kal Niranjan working with The Way of Truth, we need only navigate our mission with the contingencies of Free Will.

Universal Soul Movement

It will be The Way of Truth's development of Universal Soul Movement that will unleash the floodgate of consciousness. Universal Soul Movement reaches into the very essence of soul's wisdom and beingness. In contrast, any other form of travel soul engages in remains dependent on a teacher guiding and pointing the way to other dimensions. Universal Soul Movement unveils the God essence in soul. The aim of Universal Soul Movement is twofold: (1) to give the participant tools of individual perception and (2) to give the tools of universal perception.

The origins of Universal Soul Movement were developed through oral tradition. There is something wondrous about Universal Soul Movement, which is its transformational effect. It moves the participant from mortal consciousness to immortal consciousness, from Soul Awareness to God Awareness - and God Consciousness is not the final destination. I would like to see the participant with the vision I have seen over the horizon, over Sugmad, and experience the ecstasy of communicating with beings from other universes. Universal Soul Movement is an extension of contemplation. It is seeing without thinking, being without movement and knowing without forming questions. This is the high ground of contemplation, and it does not involve itself with movement; it is the shifting of presence IN the God Worlds.

In the early practice of contemplation, the devotee experiences the bilateral consciousness of hearing the sounds of the physical environment and experiences the sights and sounds of the Inner Worlds. It is the later stages of Universal Soul Movement that require vigilant discipline, patience, and practice. This stage involves the exclusion of the physical senses and eventual surrender to the total wisdom, power, and love of Sugmad. Universal Soul Movement requires the eviction of ego, awareness of self in the universal frame of reference and reflection, and simultaneous integration of what is seen and experienced. Reflection operates like a mirror.

Consciousness and Truth

The training awaiting the participant is not only transformative; it replaces the old consciousness with renewed perspectives. Subsequently, old patterns of thinking and behaviors fade with the engrams that have been holding themselves in cyclic movement. The Grand Council wants each of you to be God-Absorbed. This is the meaning of the word "Sehaji." The purging of impurities of your own Lower Bodies can be painful if your ego decides to hold onto what it claims as its dominion. We must "let go and become God-like." It begins with the participants asking themselves, "How can I bring more love to this event, experience, or situation?" Mohammed, following the footsteps of Jesus, whom he deeply admired, is a prime example of taking an ideal and living it. Mohammed had the purity of an open heart to receive the direct training of the Archangel Gabriel. Mohammed was not a man of high education, but his heart changed the course and shape of this Earth.

Free Will and the God Power

It is the conference of Free Will that makes the human experience divine. As a part of our human experience, we have the choice of exercising Free Will to choose whatever is or is not within the interests of all concerned. The God power works better when we act intentionally in these interests that best bring balance into fruition. When we are able to maintain balance over long periods of time, the Mental Body performs at a higher efficiency, and the God power reaches a peak in impedance as non-power, which is a manifestation of the God substance from the Eighth Plane and above.

The Soul Contract

The Soul Contract is the soul's agreement with life. It guides the participant's life experiences, personality, talents, and illnesses in its body, as well as the family environment. When the participant establishes its consciousness on the Fifth Plane and above, there is a transformation experienced by the Inner Bodies. Their spiritual signature changes, and there is a dramatic shift away from the Mental Body's influence and control. The Heart Center must be completely opened to receive the presence of Sugmad's Consciousness. The heart is the stimulus that brings forth an amendment to the Soul Contract so that soul and the Lords of Karma can come into a mutual agreement. Often soul is more stringent on its physical shell than the Lords of Karma, and this point must be clearly understood by the participant. Soul wants to insure the completion of its karmic debt and generally has little concern for the woes of its shell. This comment does not mean the physical cannot be rendered grace for emeritus service, dedication and its love for humanity. More on this subject will be made available in the spiritual manual for the Circles of the Fifth to Seventh.

Breaking Family Karma

I have done my job if the works can instill in you pureness of heart, clarity of action, and openness to Inner knowledge. Your commitment to the Light and Sound uplifts the family environment. The selfless heart permeates the entire family structure, and it can be felt throughout every room in your home. Each action we do in the interests of all concerned adjusts our karmic scroll toward the reception of grace. The Lords of Karma look kindly toward those who selflessly serve their family in a balanced way. The heart of the family members will accelerate the spiritual consciousness of the group collectively, and it is not uncommon for the entire family to join the spiritual path of the participant for this reason. The language of the heart can reach where words cannot venture. A participant of the Eighth Circle can be given the grace to escort their loved one or relative to their next spiritual assignment after their translation. A member of the Twelfth Circle and above has the right to stand before the Lords of Karma and negotiate the terms of their karmic debt. The Soul Contract opens itself to amendment and change if the heart is kept pure and the participant is completely filled with the love of Sugmad.

Changes in the Etheric Bodies

The God power attunes the Etheric Bodies to signaturize the Inner vision and Inner messages from the God Worlds. The heart is the conduit by which these messages translate themselves into sound and the written word. This aligning of the Inner Bodies infuses new intelligence to the very cellular level of the Physical Body. This is the place in time a participant can experience a healing of the heart, mind, and Physical Body. The participant emits a higher current of electrical energy than the norm after their Physical Body establishes itself in the God Worlds and can even affect electrical appliances.

Along with the changes in the Etheric Bodies come changes in the cycles by which karma is spun into the magnetic resonance. Problems and personal issues tend to resolve themselves at a higher rate of acceleration. Time also tends to move faster. The God-Realized seeker has the ability to collapse Time and Space and thereby eventually learn to collapse the cycles of energies not wanted in their life. The

Emotional Body will receive a variety of healings, taking it out of the reactionary and past engrammatic behavior that keeps the participant in feelings of inadequacy, fear, and unnecessary pain. It is at this point the Grand Council begins to make decisions about the participant's development and future spiritual mentors. The Red Dragon Order and Sri Kusulu have stepped forward to assist the participants in areas of life difficulty. Kusulu has conveyed to me his willingness to help the participants with past life information; Rumi will be coming forth to handle the transformation and matters of the heart; Pythagoras will mentor participants on intellectual enlightenment as to the physical-universal mantras for Universal Soul Movement; Milarepa will be tutoring "one-on-one" with individual participants about the keys to secret wisdom; Gopal Das will be lending a helping hand in areas of severe karmic release; and there are other Masters available who will be assigned by the Grand Council to mentor individuals in areas of specific difficulties. Sri Treylen will assist participants who are experiencing karmic instability, while Lysing will be tutoring those being considered as future Living Masters who need to pass the rigors of purification to establish themselves in the high God Worlds. Sri Leytor assists participants who are artists, writers, and adventurers of the God Worlds. He is a keeper of Sugmad's knowledge and secrets of old.

Being of the Heart

The openness of the Sacred Heart is the doorway to Universal Soul Movement and the ability to read into all aspects of life. Rumi would like to add his insights into the aforementioned with this poem:

The Heart Is the Key

"Touch the heart of those nearest you,
Speak softly of those away from you.
Hold all in the golden light of Sugmad's love,
You shall be cared for as a child of God."

~ Rumi ~

Plato

Plato has opened a vortex for the participants to speak with him about the heart, mind and body as well as secrets of the universe. You can call upon Plato by singing the spiritual name of "Dan Rin" five times and call Plato's name three times. Envision yourself speaking with Plato. Ask him any question you choose and listen to your heart. It does not matter if you do not see his face.

Ekere Tere, City of Light

Ekere Tere, City of Light, is built on a convergent labyrinth of intersecting streams of Light and Sound. The immensity of this vortex creates a wormhole effect and a high facility vehicle for soul knowledge and Universal Soul Movement. The participant who is in the city and understands "The Law of Threes" can use this wormhole to enter straight into the Sea of Love and Mercy, thus collapsing time and space and taking Soul Consciousness into Quantum Singularity. Sugmad has requested Its brightest lights to return to this life and do Its work in The Way of Truth. It has also requested the lights who founded the various paths to assist our work in the Inner Worlds. Sugmad has awakened Its brightest lights who are leading other paths to use the works of The Way of Truth to vitalize the Light and Sound essence in every path of life in our world.

The Law of Threes

Sri Kadmon

Let us start with a geometry lesson that illustrates the Law of Threes. The connection of two points in space produces a straight line, a two-dimensional image. Connecting three points in a two dimensional plane (such as a piece of paper) creates a triangle. In a two dimensional plane, various forms demonstrate no apparent difference or lessons for soul, other than shape or aesthetics, unless soul uses its powers of imagination and perception. This is why two dimensional art appeals to the abstract mind of a trained soul. Two dimensional art generally appeals to the conventional mind only if it conveys shapes known in physical planes of collective existence. In three dimensions, things change. A two-legged table has no stability; a three-legged table has more stability than two but not nearly as much as a four-legged table. Three legs on a table produce built-in movement.

A three dimensional object is exceptional due to its representing manifestation in more than two dimensional thought, which is conventional consciousness. Additionally, three dimensional perspectives convey movement, which is always essential to growth and evolution. From a three dimensional perspective, the representation of three forms is a tetrahedron, a three-sided pyramid. The intersection of two tetrahedrons produces a star tetrahedron. To extend this merging pattern into the next dimension – which would be hard to convey in the physical plane without the use of virtual reality – three tetrahedrons would intersect, forming another shape, yet unnamed, but which represents considerably more. Many souls in human form are not yet able to understand with their mind more than three dimensions. However, to begin to understand the wisdom contained in four, six, nine, and twelve dimensions is to approach the mind of Sugmad.

Universal Soul Movements can begin to unfold the mysteries of creation and Sugmad's Grand Design in lessons far exceeding geometry and physics. The mind and the Lower Worlds – the Worlds of Duality – are one of three points, rather than two points. Soul is the neutral force, as well as Divine Spirit and God. The ability to see "3" in three is the secret behind manifestation in the Physical Plane. What I am speaking of here is the reason why the participant in Ekere Tere, with this knowingness, can collapse Time and Space and be in the center of the Sea of Love and Mercy with Sugmad. Ekere Tere is a gateway leading straight into the Heart of Sugmad. It is the Power of Three that makes this Universal Soul Movement possible. It creates a wormhole effect, allowing the participant to travel into the heights of the God Worlds without effort. The aforementioned is reliant on stability, movement, and devotion. This is the foundation that gives soul reference, reflection, and resonance. All of these aspects are requirements to the acquisition of God knowledge.

The Origin of the Contemplative Technique Merkaba and Who Created It for the Light and Sound

Sri Kadmon

Many eons ago, the Masters of Antiquity, known then by other names, but of the same lineage as the Sehaji Masters today, created a contemplative technique known as the Merkaba for the purpose of ascension into the Realms of Light and Sound. The Masters of old used the technique themselves and brought it out to a handful of their select chelas to begin an infusion of the Light and Sound of Sugmad into the Mental, Causal, Astral, and Physical Realms. As a contemplative technique and as a physical form employing the Star Tetrahedron, the Merkaba was passed along to several star systems and was used by several races of beings, with variations evolving within each star system and race. However, so powerful was the technique that it was also misused in a number of self-destructive and mass-destructive ways.

The Merkaba has changed form many times and is basically a mechanical technique for lifting soul out of its physical shell via the focused motion of the mind. This technique was given to advanced and curious souls who needed to focus on a positive goal and technique to take their attention off the emphasis on activities that were taking them in the complete opposite direction of Sugmad's Heart. Without knowledge of and removal of destructive engrams, these souls returned to and continued their tendencies to love the darkness and delight in bringing pain to others. With disciplined training, these misguided initiates were able to begin to see, hear, and feel some mental level of the Light and Sound of Sugmad. They developed into Dark Magicians and used the power generated by the Merkaba to spin forces of power for evil intent, thus increasing their own destructive power. Thus, what was designed as a tool for the return to Sugmad and the power of Divine Love was abused and turned upon unsuspecting victims. The practice was withdrawn and participating souls silenced.

The Use of Merkaba

Sri Kadmon

The system of contemplation known as the Merkaba, having been used against innocent Children of Light in distant times, still carries the potential for misuse. It has here been redesigned and given for use only for the highest purpose of soul in alignment with Sugmad's Heart. Its power has been altered so that any energy sent out will come back onto the sender 1,000 times greater than when it was sent out. It will not be able to be misused for evil again without the most dire and immediate consequences to the sender. Only those with pure hearts and intent should try this powerful technique, for, if misused, it will cause serious and immediate harm. If used as directed herein, it can substantially raise the vibratory rate of the contemplator and propel him or her into the higher Inner Worlds. It can be combined with spiritual exercises of the heart, as taught by Dan Rin, to propel the consciousness of soul into the Soul Plane and beyond. First, you will need to contemplate the form of the star tetrahedron, a 3D form that represents a perfect intersection of two tetrahedrons. A tetrahedron shows perfect equality of the power of three – it is the intersection of three equilateral planes – all angles and length of sides are the same. It is best if you have a small model at hand. It can be simply made out of card stock with scissors and invisible tape. Each star tetrahedron used in the Merkaba technique is in proportion to the individual's body. It is essentially an imaginary form tailored to your size.

The New Merkaba Technique:

1. Focus on your heart and say, *"All I send out in Divine Love comes back one thousand fold. I send only love and ask to come into the Light and Sound of Sugmad."*

2. Sing the mantra, *"MER KAH BAH LA HU."* Imagine you are sitting inside a large star tetrahedron whose top point extends to an arm's length with fingers extended above your head. The bottom point would be an arm's length below the level of your feet. The forward and rear points rest at the level of your heart, again about arm's length with fingers extended.

3. Sit comfortably within the imagined shape of your personal star tetrahedron. Sing the mantra above. Get a clear sense of each tetrahedron as separate. Start each one spinning in the opposite direction – one spins to the left and the other to the right. You may start each separately to get a clear sense of it spinning before beginning the

other. It does not matter which one spins first.

4. Begin the spin slowly for the first few times you try this, to adjust to the increased vibration it creates. Spin the tetrahedrons more rapidly as you feel comfortable until they spin at the speed of light and you are lifted out of the body. You may see the energy field around you expanding to a minimum of 55 feet in diameter.

5. Remain focused in your neutral center with your heart open wide to Sugmad's Love. Take it easy with this exercise. It is very powerful.

6. Adjust to it slowly so you do not get out of balance and become ill.

7. End the exercise with, *"Blessed Be."*

How Spiritual Masters Apply the Law of Three

The Masters know that the trinity governs the foundation of their mission. They are nothing of themselves without the trinity of teacher, student, and Sugmad. There is true love and power in the interaction of this trinity. It is the Master's mission to connect the student to Sugmad and the worlds above. The "three" is a manifest unity; it magnetizes the universe into a cohesive whole. It is a marriage of creativity. Sugmad creates the seed for soul's growth, soul's consciousness expands in the physical universe from illusionary experience, and Sugmad expands from soul's expanded consciousness. The power of creation is in the "three," and it is always a continuation, like birth, growth, and rebirth. All cycles collapse into the consciousness of three.

Karma and Fear

Sugmad and the Sehaji have made the decision to purge the fear engram buried in the participant's heart. This engram is the single, strongest deterrent of the participant's ability to Universal Soul Movement. Fear is what keeps some people from making use of the grace they have been given from the Lords of Karma. It is the fear of moving forward in life because they have accepted the belief systems of others without asking themselves if they were accepting love. Fear is the absence of love and a dark cloud that paralyzes the participant into inactivity. When someone is asking you to accept their truth as your own, before you accept it into your heart, ask yourself if it will take you to a higher level of love. It is my mission to heighten your opportunity of gaining more love. It is love that purges fear and it is love that resolves the debts of life.

The Law of Neutrality

The Law of Neutrality is the Law of Non-Power and captures the essence of the God power. This law revitalizes love and is what makes life beautiful, vast, and intoxicating. It is the force that makes birds fly and opens the thirst of the mind for adventure, wisdom, freedom, and love.

The Use of Non-power

The constant practice of non-power slowly releases the negative engrams out of the magnetic resonance of the participant. This resonance is also known as the *sanskaras*, an energy wrapping around the physical body. The *sanskaras* hold the energy patterns of what causes events to occur repetitively over and over again. The cleansing of the *sanskaras* opens the participant to the positive aspects of life, drawing positive events and opportunities. Non-power causes the negative energy patterns to lose their inertia around the participant and shift to another physical host who needs other lessons in life.

The Spiritual Manuals

The road to mastership has a few rest points along the way. It is generally the Fifth and Eighth Planes. Both points are where the lessons and truths learned lay the foundation for mastership. The Eighth Circle will have its own manual due to the uniqueness of the participant's experiences in this circle. There is so much to learn on this plane, and it is a critical juncture to depart completely from the Mental Body. The complete use of the Heart Consciousness is the passkey to the Ninth Plane, the inaccessible plane.

The Importance of Babaji

The beginning of my training was an exciting adventure, and it was Babaji who was one of the first Masters that came to my side, giving me advice and good counsel on how to purge myself of latent engrams interfering with my progression into the Sea of Love and Mercy and beyond. Babaji worked with Milati as my liaison with the White Brotherhood and was instrumental in my successful agreement with the hierarchies of Brahm, Vishnu, and Shiva. In exchange for the love and assistance they pledged to The Way of Truth, I promised the services of the Lavender Order to help them keep balance in the Lower Worlds. The Order will be Heaven's gatekeepers, assisting Kal Niranjan's angels of light and darkness in their enforcement of the spiritual laws in the Lower Worlds as well as assisting Sri Tindor Saki in the maintenance of the universal vortices. The Way of Truth and its participants are surrounded by the love and protection of countless Masters. This is a message Babaji wanted me to convey to you, and these two passages came from the book called, *Babaji, The Beginning Has No End,* my spiritual dialogue with this Master of old.

Babaji's Message to The Way of Truth

Yours is a mission of great merit. I, Babaji, an acknowledged Master in the way of the Light and Sound, say to you that you have opened the consciousness of many souls to this new beginning. I offer my assistance and blessings to this journey in all ways, as before, in my journeys as a Master to many others that have brought the message of love to the hearts of those that sought to feel the presence of God on this Earth. I have laid down a foundation of spiritual interest that has been hidden from the hearts of many, but once again is being felt in this universe. The key for this compelling process of enlightenment is that the Light and Sound in this universe has gained a new strength. It has been felt in many of the Higher Realms of Beingness as you in The Way of Truth have changed the frequency to make it more available to all souls that are being awakened in your efforts to please this Sugmad. The souls that have flocked to the entrances of these new vortices of spiritual energy will truly find the beginning that has no end. It is a necessity in this Sugmad to join all prior and future efforts to sing out to all souls that God is ever present in all of them if they seek love amongst all people and ways of spiritual awakening. In years past, the message has been placed in the hands of many devout people who were led astray by the intensity of the new God power that has been placed in this universe. They sought to direct it in the ways of the Mental Body and ego, and not through the way of the Sacred Heart. As I saw these things beginning to happen, I asked the great Overlords of this universe to provide a release valve for this restrained energy, as they could also see the constriction of the Light and Sound, and the uncomfortable state of being in Sugmad's Heart as souls were being held back from experiencing this wondrous love of life and Spirit. The Way of Truth was set before the Council, and a representative was selected in Dan Rin, who, once put through a rigorous cleansing and training, was offered and accepted the honor of bringing this new balance to all souls who seek the true, selfless love in the God Worlds and wish to share Sugmad's grace in all expressions of spiritual life.

It is for you to take hold of this God power and process through the Light and Sound that which is in transformation into an accessible set of new engrams that all willing souls may take this journey. The clarity of the Light of God in your heart will shine brightly as in times of old, when angels spoke directly to all souls of the open, selfless heart who knew of and sought a connection to God's love in this universe. I thank you for your commitment and love for Sugmad and the Grand Council. If you look within your Heart, you will find me there.

~ Sri Michael

Dedication of the Universal Vortex

Pinetop, Arizona Retreat

July 9-10, 2005

The Pinetop, Arizona Dedication of the Universal Vortex

I would like to welcome each of you to this dedication of the Universal vortex of the Light and Sound and acknowledgement of its new seat and assignment with the Universe and Sugmad. There are many Masters with us this day commending each of you for your commitment to the mission set forth by the Grand Council.

The three aspects of Spirit are love, wisdom, and power. With wisdom, you can become the seer who wanders the Earth, spouting wise words with an elevation of ego. With power, you can become an authority over those who are still unsure of their spiritual identity and their Father's inheritance. But this is the blind leading the blind, much like the flock without a true and loving shepherd. Power and wisdom cannot stand on hallowed ground without love. Of the three aspects, it is love and love alone that is the essence of the Heart Consciousness. This is the greatest and most valuable of the three aspects. Love is the key that unlocks Higher Realms, power is the strength to climb the stairs of Heaven, and wisdom is the sight and knowledge to understand the proper way to proceed once the Gates of

Heaven have been won. The Heart Consciousness leads the soul to greater heights and understanding of the ways of Spirit.

Sri Leytor and *The Way of Truth Eternal - Book I*

Sri Leytor, chief architect and spiritual consultant of the holy book, *The Way of Truth Eternal, Book I* (hereinafter referred to as *Book I*), wants each of us to revisit the contents of this book. Sri Leytor feels that its contents have not been fully digested and understood by the participant, the God seeker standing at the Summit of God Consciousness. He and the Sehaji do not want the participants to become spiritual consumers, running from one book to another, without understanding the gems of love and wisdom embedded within them.

Sri Leytor was chosen by Milarepa to finalize my research on *Book I*, and it was truly a privilege to have this Master tutoring me in the spiritual high ground of the Sehaji. Sri Leytor is a member of the Grey Robe Tradition, yet wears many other robes of the various orders to fulfill his mission. He honors all the various orders such as: The Green and Brown Robes, who keep the Physical and Lower Worlds beautiful and in balanced growth. The White Robes tutor souls ready to enter Sugmad's realms of unity and into Its Heart. The Beige Robes maintain the secret works of the universe. The Lavender Robes maintain the flow of balance and healing above and below the Great Divide of Sugmad. Sri Leytor does not want you, once a Master in your own right, trembling at the Gates of Heaven. Many God seekers spend lifetimes trembling at Heaven's doors fearful of being unworthy of admission, carrying guilt, negative engrams, and memories of their pasts. The true case of many initiates of the Fifth and Eighth Circles is their inability to let go of their dependency on human consciousness and ego. The aforementioned leaves a firm grip on their unwillingness to release the shortsighted teachings of holy men and gurus who make the heavenly worlds unreachable.

Vigilant Study of the Spiritual Literature

Heaven is here and now and within your grasp. You must diligently stay within the focused study of the discourses, *Book I*, and the spiritual manuals and place tremendous study on the upcoming books: *Ekere Tere, City of Light* and *Babaji, The Beginning Has No End*. These will be studied in a class environment due to the immensity of their spiritual vibration.

Sri Leytor's Mission

It is Sri Leytor's mission to gather and disseminate the knowledge and wisdom of Sugmad's universe. He has transcended and moved beyond the laws of the planes and universes and also is in multiple places at one time. It is part of his mission to help the participants of The Way of Truth to move beyond their perceived limitations. The offering of Sri Leytor's services to us is but a tip of the iceberg coming our way. Leytor said, "I will reach out to participants in their contemplations, private journals and in their spiritual classes." Sri Leytor is a reflection of the many Masters standing ready to serve this Earth with the attitude that learning and love is reciprocal in nature. The Masters also learn from you as much as you learn from them. Leytor is known as a universal traveler and researcher and gathers the wisdom of many civilizations in far-off star systems and realms above. He is the attaché of the Grand Council and often reports directly to Milarepa. Leytor also carries valuable communications between the masterships and sets up assemblies and forums of exchange. Leytor has guided Dan Rin to many unknown and least known temples and libraries for his research into the secret works of Spirit.

Sri Leytor and the Lavender Robe Order

Leytor has assisted in the construction of the Lavender Robe Order. He feels the Order offers an exceptional contribution to the universe. Doctors and healing professionals in this day are not well equipped to handle the depth of karmic constipation and blockage found in many souls who have evolved spiritually and emotionally but have not been able to clear their physical vehicles. Healing has a multidimensional framework that modern science is yet to understand, and has appeared unwilling to go outside the scope of its limited knowledge. The Lavender Robes of the highest degree will be able to converse with the Lords of Karma about an illness to assess the level of remedy being given without the cost of additional karma. They will be able to look at the root cause element of the illness. Prophecy will not be permitted without the full consent of its head Abbot.

The Lavender Robes will be the peacemakers, mediators, and spiritual counselors who will often be the consuls for those who need a confidential ear regarding a life situation. They practice Universal Soul Movement and are those who ride the spiritual frontiers assisting Kal Niranjan in the administering of balance in the Lower Divide of the universe. The jurisdiction of the Lavender Robes will vary with their soul and skill development. Many seekers of Light will come from other paths of life to receive their training in this Order, to restore the vibrancy of the Light and Sound in the belief system they represent. In this way, the sons and daughters of God will feed the spiritually hungry and uplift the hearts of those in suffering.

The gates of God-Realization are universally open to individuals of all walks of life, and their obtainment is reliant on the individual's soul development and spiritual training from other lifetimes.

Studying *The Way of Truth Eternal - Book I*

The literal scope of the holy *Book I* is but a fraction of the whole; it is what is released within the reader once its pages are read. *Book I* activates participants spiritual signatures and lends guidance to their Soul Contracts, especially so if their hearts are ready, and pure and devoid of the mind's luggage. The secrets it reveals are those already locked in the heart consciousness. *Book I* is to be viewed as a key. The virtues of compassion, diligence, focus, discernment, persistence, and, most of all, patience ~ will awaken the knowledge of the God power, the non-power in your life. The exercise of spiritual freedom also means releasing the collectivity of one's fears and concepts of limitation. Dear participants, exercise the freedom gifted to you in The Way of Truth and replace your individual consciousness with that of the universal consciousness! *Book I*'s terms, names of Masters and spiritual cities are all keys for opening up vortices and can be used as mantras in your daily contemplations.

The Spiritual City of Arhirit on the Etheric Plane

The city of Arhirit is a hub of academic study of the arts, literature, mathematics, and esoteric sciences. I have visited the City to hear its instructors speak and debate on issues of the Lower Divide. Entrance requires a guide of spiritual merit and accessibility is granted on the soul's development of the Heart Consciousness. A wormhole vortex of Light and Sound resides in the city that is a direct portal to the Court of Sat Nam. The Guardian of this city is Saguna Brahm. Spiritual records are kept on every soul who has employed Universal Soul Movement to visit and lecture within its walls. This is an amazing city of love and wisdom that simply goes beyond the wealth of our imagination. Many of the visitors often go to Ekere Tere to continue their studies and training.

Ekere Tere, City of Light

Ekere Tere is an extension of Arhirit, a satellite station of learning. The vortices of both cities are connected, and those of you who enter Ekere Tere will eventually be going to Arhirit for advanced esoteric studies. Besides the aforementioned vortices, Leytor said there are countless interconnecting vortices now in place for your facility of spiritual growth and Universal Soul Movement. The job now is to get the individual consciousness freed up of its dross, and the key to your universal visitations will be reliant on your vigilant study of the works at hand and your daily contemplative exercises. The cries of Africa's suffering called for Ekere Tere's construction. I have read the experiences of the many participants who visited and passed through its gates. Some are frequent visitors and temporary residents receiving training from the Lavender Robes and individual tutors who teach the secrets of creative manifestation and Quantum Universality. Africa's cries have been heard, and the Sehaji responded with the building of Ekere Tere. Ekere Tere was primarily built for the souls of Africa where life is so harsh and stripped of all illusion of safety and permanency in the Lower Worlds. It is a springboard to all other spiritual cities and temples of higher esoteric learning. Only souls with purity of heart will be able to see and enter into Ekere Tere or any of its interconnections.

The power of black magic has been dealt with; its demi-gods and Dark Lords have been dispatched to greener pastures. The current of dark power has been disconnected, and the only remnant of influence left is the residual fear in the hearts of those who have witnessed the wrath of black magic. There is also a residue of fear in the Inner Bodies, emotions, and minds due to karmic patterns and frequencies. Africa, this planet's heart, is now in the process of healing, and the severities of any present pains are due to facsimiles residing in its consciousness. The African Renaissance has now begun and the pace of the changes depends on the willingness of the diverse groups and tribal consciousnesses to progress forward. Africa, in some sense, has successfully been through a quadruple bypass surgery. Those who are attending the classes will be getting further adjustments on their Etheric Bodies in the City of Arhirit.

Using the Universal Soul Movement Technique to Visit the Spiritual Cities

1. When you are rested and have at least one-half hour completely undisturbed, sit in a comfortable position. You may play relaxing music or sing any of the sacred words or sounds that have helped you in the past to enter into realms above.

2. Relax and envision your heart wide open as never before.

3. Call to Our Lord, Sugmad, and in these or your own words, say: *"Sugmad, I declare myself to be your loving devoted vehicle for divine love now and evermore. Please send*

> *me a helper, Dan Rin, another Sehaji*
> *Master or angel, to escort me to the city of*
> *Ekere Tere, then on to _____ (your*
> *desired final destination.)"*

A significant part of this process of Universal Soul Movement to Ekere Tere is complete surrender. What good does it do to go where you have not consciously gone before and try to remain in full control? The River of Life is wild and free. So, too, must you be to enter into it.

Remember that Sugmad loves you and bolsters you. Let go of control and join with Masters of old who have already gone where you seek and know of methods they are willing to teach you. Trust is not easy for many souls in the Physical Realms, but trust is essential to journey in the Inner Realms. So, trust!

Stay awake and receptive to the tiniest of nuances. Allow the mind to rest, or, for best results, send the Mental Body out to work on other tasks while you, Soul, contemplate, as is taught by Dan Rin in other writings. Trust in Sugmad, in the Sehaji Masters, and in the process of unfoldment is essential and cannot be emphasized enough.

So to summarize:

1. Set up your physical, emotional, mental and spiritual consciousness;

2. Declare your intentions and ask for guidance;

3. Relax;

4. Trust;

5. Join with the unity of souls who have walked The Way of Truth;

5. Enjoy your experience!

6. Repeat!

7. End the exercise with, "Blessed Be."

The Law of Assumption

The Law of Assumption reigns in the Lower Worlds of Beingness. This law acknowledges the power of the Holy Spirit as it is formed in realms above and is given to souls to manipulate through their individual bodies and beingness. Descartes declared a partial truth, "I think, therefore I am." Quantum Physics and Chaos Theory acknowledge the connection with the intentions or assumptions of the observer and that of the physical matter being observed. What people assume and expect, actually colors and creates the framework and boundaries of their reality. Few people are aware of much outside of their accepted personal assumptions. A paradigm shift in consciousness must be made for soul to see the world in another way. We can choose what will hold us hostage or what will set us free. Our assumptions act as a filter for what we see and feel, then influence what we think and how we act. The illusions of the Lower Worlds tend to hold us captive here. It is all illusion, but you can choose the illusions you want to experience. There is far more to life than the Physical Plane. Remember the raw power of love and how it feels to love and be loved. Whatever you hold in your consciousness eventually hardens itself into your truth and your Outer reality. Make your choices and responsibility a constant area of focus and attention in order to gain dominion over yourself.

The Rejuvenation Process of The Way of Truth and the Power of Initiation

In these Physical Worlds of Duality, nothing exists without its equal and opposite counterpart. There cannot be action without rest, aging without youth, or heat without cold; the polarities are non-ending. Motion is a necessity of life in the physical world. The gist is to get motion to its fullest spectrum within the participant. This movement is a conscious expansion that widens the participant's scope of acceptance and love. If the participants of The Way of Truth want to know God and live in the God-Absorbed state, then they must become rejuvenated in all their Inner Bodies and in all areas of consciousness in order to transition from the human to God Consciousness.

In the God Worlds, soul is in a continual state of knowingness and is creatively attempting to communicate with its Lower Body counterparts "moment by moment." The Lower Bodies must be placed into alignment to receive the full flow of Spirit ushering Itself from the God Worlds through the *pritraya* of soul (that part of soul that serves the

Holy Spirit and fulfills Best-Laid Plans.) Spirit then passes through the Crown Chakra located at the top of the head (the thousand-petaled lotus) to the lower chakras of the body. The purpose of the Rejuvenation process is to refresh, revitalize, renew, and regenerate all the Inner Bodies into a state of balance. Many members of other paths, with a lapsed connection to the spiritual energies, have been running their engines on half-empty tanks and old pistons without being fully aware of their failing Inner structures. They knew something was wrong and that nothing was working in life for them. The repetitive circumstances of life appeared cyclically infinite, like a groove on a record that keeps spinning. The Rejuvenation process brings back the resiliency of youth and reawakens the fullness of life's perpetuation in the physical, emotional, karmic, mental, intuitive, and spiritual lives.

Initiation in The Way of Truth is not merely a ritual; it is a physical manifestation. The Rejuvenation process is like the use of fertilizer in a garden before seed is planted. The Sehaji want to insure that the "inflow and outflow" is equal in reciprocity and movement, and the mental consciousness cannot prepare the participant for the flow of Spirit and positive changes that come with it. The spiritual flow must be gentle at first and then is slowly increased as the participant gains an understanding of the gifts that have been given. Even with this pacing of inflow, the God seeker could still be somewhat overwhelmed. The idea is to build the confidence of the participants as they grow spiritually. Dan Rin has made spiritual manuals available for the seekers to decide what they want to learn and focus on as they expand in consciousness from the viewpoint of strength and balance.

The Trials of Fire and Water

It is fear and oftentimes ignorance that keeps souls from embarking on the journey home to God. The Second Initiation is a vital step forward in this journey and opens a gateway that will never be closed. Once the Second Initiation is given, the Gates of Eternity are opened and remain so. The journey on this road less traveled has begun, and the soil must be turned to plant seed for harvest. Tests are devised to turn back those of a curious nature or those who have weakness of character and are given to strengthen the courage, confidence, and mettle of the God seeker. The aspirant must use what they learn in the first few years of initiation. Do not be discouraged if tests are failed. Get up and keep moving forward. There is nothing to lose but ignorance.

Self-surrender

Character traits of the little self have no place in the God Worlds. The tools of mental consciousness used to lord over others will deter and undermine the God seeker's climb up to the summit of God Consciousness. Surrender of this little self is the relinquishing of unnecessary weight as we journey toward the Godhead. Be focused on discernment and loving devotion. Surrender comes with patience, devotion, courage, and practice of the daily contemplative exercises. The bustling and minute-by-minute traffic of our daily lives gives us clues as to the best approach for individual surrender to the flow of God's wisdom and love. Listen to the very sounds of the world around you. They are the living creations of others. Allow your heart to interpret the meaning of what you hear. Remember the voicing of the heart is much softer than the ramblings of the mind. It is important to understand that knowing the ways of the heart is knowing God.

Living with Heart

Knowing the ways of the heart is knowing God. God gives us life through Its love. Unconditional Divine Love is the way of the heart and The Way of Truth. The melody of life is sung in every moment, and love is the key to understanding the joy and ecstasy in it. Closing the door of love's opportunity is closing your heart to God. Look for the divine expression of love in every moment, every molecule and aspect of your life and environment. Heart is the communication essence of our true beingness in soul and is the point from where we can experience the richness of life. In my daily duties, I hear the multitude of obstacles facing our participants and the members of other paths. Most of their concerns issue from the mind, and I find once I can shift their attention from the mind to their heart, what is standing behind the obstacles becomes prominently clear. Respond to life's trials with answers charged with the Light and Sound of Sugmad and reflect the Breath of God in your actions. Be focused on the journey of soul through this human life process that enriches the quantity and quality of heart energy that charges our existence in this Plane and Higher Realms.

Let us learn the lessons of Lemuria and Atlantis. The ego consciousness of these two great civilizations drove them spirally downward into self-destructive impulses and the need to control nature and change the evolutionary expression of genetics and physics. When the mind dominates a civilization, its end is imminent, and it leaves no true quality of beauty and wonderment behind it. Be One with the God essence within you, and it will touch those you love and those who affect your life in unseen ways. Love is the only emotion that connects you, the God seeker, to your highest potential. Learn life knowing that the love from your heart is the one thing you can take with you when you leave this Physical Body and you will SEE God in every aspect of your life.

Allow Your Heart to be Seen

Our human experience is multidimensional, and we are moving our Inner Bodies into the Higher Worlds in Universal Soul Movement. Let the souls who reside on other levels of consciousness SEE your heart first in your personal inquiries of self-discovery and the Lords of Karma will render you Grace, Dharma, and the pass-key of entry to endless worlds of existence. Our hearts resonate with a harmonic signature that can be seen, felt, and recognized on the Astral Plane and above. Heart consciousness opens doors, portals, and wormholes in accordance with the calibration and purity of our hearts.

The nine-pointed tetrahedron, the spiritual symbol of The Way of Truth, is a mantra that is the unified Light and Sound code for Universal Soul Movement. Participants of The Way of Truth from other planets use our logo as the mantra to journey to the City of Light, Ekere Tere. They place the logo in their Middle Eye, and it transports them to the spiritual class or tutorial they are seeking to attend. The Tetrahedron, once placed and focused upon, emanates the internal sound of the Trinity, the Code of Three and its higher expressions. It is a perceptual filter for Universal Soul Movement. Focus on it as you go through your day, as when communicating with others, and in silent contemplation, it harnesses the God power within it.

A Universal Soul Movement Exercise

Completely relax, feel and see your Inward and Outward devotion to Sugmad and sing the secret name for God, "**HU**," for a few minutes.

1. Now begin to visualize The Way of Truth logo. Once it becomes clear in your Inner vision and Middle Eye, then proceed to the next step.

2. Here you may see what you want to fulfill in your day, in your life, or ask the

questions you would like to have answered. Allow this to continue for at least 15 minutes and just flow with the pictures and Inner voices. Imagine hearing birds singing their songs of praise in this joyous moment. Allow the quietude to give you bliss and inexplicable feelings of love.

3. Fill yourself with the love of Sugmad. State three times, inwardly or outwardly, *"I operate through the consciousness of Sugmad."*

4. Try this exercise now with a *"HU"* for at least three minutes.

5. End the exercise with, "Blessed Be."

(The attendees then performed the exercise.)

When you hold the Tetrahedron in your mind's eye, you are in Quantum Singularity, harnessing the highest elements of non-power.

The Love of the Nine-pointed Tetrahedron

The Tetrahedron is foundational to Paulji's (Sri Paul Twitchell's, Peddar Zaskq's) writing in his book on prophecy and also to the use of Universal Soul Movement to move back and forward on the Time Track. Universal Soul Movement on the Time Track is primarily holographic, and the souls we speak with from different time periods are safeguarded from having their consciousness changed from their exposure to the knowledge of our time period. Time is a sequence of events, and if altered even slightly, can change a multitude of destinies and Soul Contracts. It is imperative that knowing your potential future requires absolute detachment and discipline, and this is why so few are granted this form of Universal Soul Movement.

The harmonic signature of soul is also what grants access to the knowledge of the wisdom temples. This is the reason why the Inner and Outer Master has structured the Rejuvenation process and initiatory movement as a slow, loving alignment of the Inner Bodies. A premature initiation may slow down the conscious expression of soul and thus create imbalance and an exaggerated ego. These types of soul are held in abeyance from the God Worlds until they learn humility. They will be amongst those souls trembling at the Gates of Heaven.

How to Measure the True Intent of Another's Heart

To access the purity of another's heart, listen to how many times they say "I" in their important conversations with you. When you first find a person whose presence sprinkles the seed of love, go into contemplation and use any mantra of choice. Then in contemplation visualize their face in your Middle Eye. Once their face is crystallized in your Middle Eye, ask "Are you here to collect a debt? Are you here to pay back a debt? Are you here for mutual love, respect, and true friendship?" Collection and the repayment of debts are in the mire of illusion, and both lead to highly-complex relationships. These complex relationships might be thick in intimate excitement but deep in karmic debt. The way of mutual love, love, and true friendship is generally the way to go unless you need a spiritual lesson. The message from soul is generally clearer if this contemplation is done several times before any physical intimacy has occurred. Once the waters of soul have touched the scent of human passion, the voice of soul will soften with the promise of what you want rather than what you are really receiving. In time, what is sweet can turn into a bitter, lukewarm burden of emotional regret and eventual pain.

Keeping Our Hearts Connected to Sugmad

We have to keep asking ourselves if we are staying in balance with the flow of Spirit and Sugmad's Will. The question alone is the stimulating action for Spirit to shift its energy in some way to foster greater balance. Soul knows when Its physical counterpart is out of balance. Also the act of devotion to Its cause, which is one of the highest forms of caring, will always guide the pure of heart to the place of acceptance of merging with the center of Sugmad's heart. It is our conscious effort to walk as Masters in our own right that fuels the motivation to keep compassion and selflessness in our hearts.

Having the Heart of a Spiritual Warrior

We are the lights of Sugmad's love. We must be the beacons that will guide those still in the darkness and those still in slumber. Those souls in spiritual recline need the lights to point the way to break the karmic cycles of those whose hearts are ready to make the journey [home to Sugmad.] We carry Sugmad's Sword with the recalibrated energies of the new path of the Light and Sound to relieve the unnecessary suffering and imbalances of this world.

Every morning say this postulate:

The Heart of a Spiritual Warrior

"Sugmad is my sword
The Living Master is my Shield
The Holy Spirit is my Armor
And the Sehaji is my guidance
into the Light and Sound of God."

Afterwards sing *"HU"* five times and meet the challenges of your day!

A poem to read in times of stress and need — A gift from Sugmad

"O Sugmad,
Allow me to rest my mind from its needs.

Bring to my heart understanding.
Let the eye of my soul see the grace of your wisdom
in all that transpires.
Let me give from the infinite Love that is my beginning.
May compassion be the way of my thoughts.
May forgiveness be the breadth of my feelings.
Bring those not yet awakened to Your Peace and
give them rest from their fears.
Let every effort of my being be that of infinite love.
Let the day be that of the highest order of grace.
And O Sugmad, allow me to be like HU."

Dear Participants, I am and will always be with each of you. Thank you for your love, support, and commitment to the spiritual mission of Sugmad, the Grand Council, and the Living Sehaji Master.

~ Sri Michael

"Climbing the Summit to God Consciousness"

Columbia, Maryland Universal Retreat

August 10, 13 and 14, 2005

Wednesday Evening Session, August 10, 2005

The Giving of the Universal Darshan

I want to thank each of you for your presence, love, and support of The Way of Truth. The Way of Truth is a mystery school and a path constructed of the highest secrets and esoteric knowledge of God. It is a road back to God-Realization, and it is maintained and protected by an ancient order of Masters, who have existed on Earth and the Inner Realms since this universe was created. Throughout history, and the numerous civilizations of humanity, this mystery school and brotherhood had been known under different names, at different times; such as the philosophical schools of Plato, Aristotle and Parmenides and Pythagoras; the Sufis under Shamus Tabriz and Rumi; and Dionysus and Mithra. Regardless of their names and the times they revealed themselves, these former paths of the Light and Sound led souls beyond the Worlds of Illusion and into the God Worlds. In recent times, these Masters have been known as the Brotherhood of the Sehaji Masters of the Celestial Seas, and its present day leader is called the Living Sehaji Master.

The presentation tonight is the forefront talk of The Way of Truth Universal Retreat in Columbia, Maryland. Many Masters of this universe have pledged themselves to working with the participants in their dream states and in assisting them in reaching the higher rungs of the God Worlds. I am fortunate to have these great avatars with me and you to represent this large shift in universal consciousness. Those who are ready to connect with the Light and Sound of God and want to experience God-Realization will simply find themselves at our doors through the lead of Spirit. I have been tutored and trained in the ancient mysteries by many Masters of various cultural traditions. All of the Masters were teachers of the Light and Sound of God. Two Masters who were at the beginning of my physical training for the Rod of Power, my mantle of leadership of The Way of Truth, are Milati and Babaji. Milati awakened me to the creative forces behind Sugmad and the other spiritual hierarchies. Babaji instructed me on the chakric system, the power centers of the body and how these centers play a divine role in our unfoldment to God-Realization.

I received the mantle of my leadership from an ancient teacher named Milarepa. He sits at the helm of a Spiritual Council in the God Worlds that guides and advises me in the direction of how the Light and Sound is distributed on Earth and other places of the universe. There have been other spiritual teachers before me in this tradition and some represent other paths that housed the life code of existence called "HU." The HU is now housed with The Way of Truth.

The God seekers of The Way of Truth contemplate every day. They gently sing inwardly and outwardly the word HU as a spiritual word of choice, while their eyes are closed, sitting on an easy chair, or place of comfort. Those who contemplate focus on their Middle Eye, that space between the eyebrows called the pineal gland. The Middle Eye is a doorway that soul opens to begin its Universal Soul Movement into the worlds beyond the physical veil. It opens the spiritual connection between the practitioner and a greater flow of Spirit.

The Way of Truth has been given the duty of increasing the frequency of love in this universe. This path of life has kept its doors open to seekers of truth and has adjusted the Light and Sound to accommodate the needs of all who thirst for the heavenly waters. In The Way of Truth, we call "God" also by its ancient name "Sugmad." This term represents a spiritual vibration that has never been profaned or compromised. The Way of Truth wants to provide each and every seeker with the opportunity of reaching God-Realization. The intent is to break the wheel of reincarnation and be afforded the Grace to journey further into higher states of God-Absorption. This is achieved through The Way of Truth's monthly discourses, study of the spiritual manuals and books, and living life from the highest aspects of spiritual and material survival. This perspective allows soul to release its negative weight, and the wondrous sheen of soul's light begins to naturally glow and permeate the seeker's countenance.

Why The Way of Truth is a Mystery School

The Way of Truth as a mystery school means there is no strict adherence to doctrine and organizational rules. Everything the God seeker experiences is considered important to their growth along the path, for it is love that is the most powerful ingredient for healing and spiritual expansion for soul's development. The foundation of learning is structured on the discourses and the Inner guidance of the various Masters of The Way of Truth. The idea is to bring you to the understanding of your true self. Many areas of universal understanding have remained a mystery until now. Many have gained insight beyond the veil of the unknown by opening their heart to the Light and Sound. We are shifting the paradigm of questions from "why" to "how" and are providing God seekers with spiritual exercises to develop a greater understanding of their lives, families, beloveds, and their livelihoods.

The Uniqueness of The Way of Truth

The intense driving purpose of this path is to resurrect the essence of the Light and Sound in all walks of life. It is also our purpose to give seekers the opportunity and the means to read their own Life Contracts. The Masters of the Sehaji are in continual conference with the Living Sehaji Master about the distribution of our teachings and the way and manner they envision its message to be constructed and thereby presented to the world.

Self-Realization and God-Realization

It is my mission to guide each participant of The Way of Truth to the state of consciousness known as Self-Realization and God-Realization. Self-Realization means understanding yourself and your highest aspect as soul. It is the heart opening to Soul Awareness. God seekers can tune into the workings of their lives and change the course of what is contingently agreed upon with the Lords of Karma. God seekers are changing their lives and are becoming the captains and commanders of their own destinies. The term relative to this state of consciousness is called "Quantum Singularity," which is being able to see yourself in all things. God-Realization is being in that state of consciousness in which God, also known as Sugmad, operates through the participant as a conscious vehicle for Its works. This state allows the perception whereby there is no separation of its consciousness and all of existence. The term that best describes this state is "Quantum Universality." It affords the knowing that in ultimate reality you and God are united in all acts of human creativity.

As soul, the entire universe is our home. This viewpoint can be experienced through the contemplative exercises provided in *The Way of Truth Eternal, Book I,* the spiritual discourses, and the upcoming books near completion: *Babaji, The Beginning Has No End* and *Ekere Tere, City of Light.* The physical shell is given to soul for experience and the gaining of love and wisdom.

How you choose to discern and interpret the living of life is your choice. You choose the reality you experience. You choose the responsibilities gathered in life. If you do not make productive choices for yourself, someone with more consciousness will make them for you. Making the proactive connection with God's love yields more love for you and a multiplicity of significant other experiences. Exercise the spiritual freedom you have been given, recognize choice as the God-given extension of Free Will, and you will find the high spiritual ground within yourself. Below is a short spiritual exercise I would like to share with you. It is a method to connect with Spirit and God in a proactive way.

A Spiritual Exercise

1. Let us close our eyes, relax, and slowly focus on the Middle Eye.

2. You may ask questions about your day or about life situations posing some type of challenge to you in the quietude of this portion of the contemplation.

3. Sing *"HU"* five times, allow quietude, and let the pictures of the mind flow through your consciousness for about five minutes. The pictures represent soul speaking to you through symbols.

4. Say (inwardly or outwardly) *"I operate from the heart consciousness of Sugmad"*

three times and then allow quietude. Soul will let you know when the contemplation is over.

5. End the exercise with, *"Blessed Be."*

You have my love, blessings, and Darshan.

~ Sri Michael

Friday Evening Session, August 12, 2005

The Sehaji Vision of the Universal Healer

My talk with you tonight was inspired by my interaction with Jesus' teacher, Zadok. Besides Jesus' continual contact and assistance from the Archangel Gabriel, Zadok was singularly the human teacher that imparted Jesus' valuable knowledge about the mysteries of life and death. Zadok was a member of the Grey Robe tradition of the Sehaji. At the time he chose Jesus as a student, Zadok decided to be his primary teacher for his mission to raise the consciousness of humanity. Life was harsh and cruel during the Roman occupation, and Israel was considered one of the most undesirable places to live in the Roman Empire. The countryside was overrun by bandits, the cities were mercilessly ruled by Rome and the Jewish nobility called the Sanhedrin. Men of wisdom had to be careful with their words and skillful in the art of secrecy, invisibility, and the Law of Silence.

Master Zadok developed Jesus' creativity in the art of healthy living, healing, and resurrection. Under the guidance of Zadok the art of resurrection was carried out in absolute secrecy. He advised Jesus against any public displays. Zadok felt certain healings were in the universal balance, in consideration of the harsh times they lived in and the lack of medical knowledge. Nonetheless, he knew healing was still on the razor's edge, and Zadok suspected Jesus would not keep the healing arts out of the watchful eyes of the Sanhedrin. Zadok found Jesus a total delight to teach, and he had unbounded love and enthusiasm for the acquiring of knowledge. Jesus would contemplate as he worked with his hands and loved to carve wooden sculptures for those he loved. The very ground Jesus walked on was magnetized with his love for all life. Jesus acknowledged no boundaries between man and woman. This aspect was his greatest strength and his greatest weakness. He was often unable to see treachery in others. He only recognized the highest good in all. In Zadok's words and understanding, Jesus did take on the karma of others, but his motive was pure love. Unfortunately, Zadok did not instruct Jesus on how to communicate with the Lords of Karma regarding the shifting of karmic-related energy. Another concern Zadok had regarding Jesus' well-being was his not putting any attention on his physical protection and his not seeing the threat he posed to Judaic authorities and the fear consciousness building in his disciples; plus he did not pay attention to how those of theological authority in times to come would attempt to control his message of love. The Universal Healer is connected to the heart of humanity, and the Lavender Robe is connected to the Heart of God and Its universe. Jesus felt a sense of loss, knowing his end would come barely into his thirties and before he reached full spiritual strength, for his disciples were far from being properly trained.

The Art of Molecular Transformation

Jesus was experienced in Universal Soul Movement at birth. In order to learn the Art of Molecular Transformation, he had to be skilled at Universal Soul Movement. Jesus came to Earth to expand the awareness of man's Inner Bodies and their capabilities to handle the higher frequencies of Light and Sound. When Jesus raised Lazarus from the dead, he also raised a great deal of fear toward his teachings. He wanted to teach people how to heal themselves. Jesus was truly a Universal Healer, and he was a defender of women's rights in that day. Jesus did not want man's ego to stand in the way of women's attainment of God-Realization. Many participants of The Way of Truth lived in that day and time.

The secret group of mystics called the Essenes recruited Jesus' parents, Joseph and Mary, into their order. They insured that Joseph and Mary's Soul Contracts were in alignment with bringing Jesus to conception and into their care. The strength of the Essenes was in their development of intuition, initiation and their strict adherence to the Law of Silence. The Essenes began to withdraw their presence from Jesus' side when his evangelism became too well known. They considered Jesus' approach to spiritual upliftment of the masses on the edge and risky. He could not hide his great love for humanity. All he touched became a testimony to this great love.

The Master Vision of the Lavender Robe Order

The aim of the Lavender Robe Order is to give the true secret of what is healing in the hands of the God seeker. This order will also show humanity practical ways of attaining God-Absorption, and this will result in the development of higher living skills. The Order's membership will come from various healing professions, like clergy from other paths, medical doctors, psychiatrists, chiropractors, massage and occupational therapists, naturopathic doctors, teachers, social workers, theatrical professionals, and many others. This order wants those who are striving toward the goal of Sehaji Mastership within its ranks and who will know how to live in the God-Realized state at all times. They will be astute in the knowledge of the Inner and Outer Bodies of humankind. The Lavender Robe will be able to understand the karmic relationship between history, attitudes, facsimiles, and recreations of the individual soul. Along with the aforementioned would be the ability of reading Soul Records, with permission. The Order would also be able to meet with the Lords of Karma and renegotiate an individual's Soul Contract for the resolution of a debt. There will be Lavender Robes located all over the world, regulating vortices of Light and Sound, serving as channels for the Grand Council and Sugmad. Zadok forfeited his life making the dream of the Lavender Order a reality. Like

Jesus, he saw his life somewhat inconsequential in value next to the spiritual upliftment of the world and the universe. Zadok's association with Jesus made him endlessly sought after by the Romans and their colonial armies. The wounds Zadok suffered far exceeded Jesus' afflictions, but he foresaw his end. Zadok's foresight stimulated his training of Fubbi Quantz, who became the next Living Master.

Zadok promises to those who come to him for spiritual instruction that he will be teaching those healing modalities, Universal Soul Movement exercises, and is also willing to give instruction in areas of specific interest. The Universal Healers, like St. Francis and St. Catherine of Siena, represent those great avatars who perceived their mission with connecting those in suffering with the Light and Sound first, and, secondly, speaking with the Lords of Karma as to what they can change and cannot change. What is greater than our salvation? What is greater than having Sugmad's love and grace? Healing always begins in the heart. We must allow Spirit to heal the wounds of the heart. The God seeker must see the entirety of their constitution like a garden. Do not turn the soil to see the fruits of what you have planted. TEND TO YOUR LIFE AS A GARDEN, GIVING YOUR LOVE OF LIFE'S BEAUTY AND DO NOT EXPECT ANYTHING BACK. LIFE WILL REWARD YOU.

Healing is multidimensional, and often the source of a malady is on the Astral, Causal, or Mental Planes. Observe how you speak about yourself, and then go within to SEE what you need to change, and, most importantly, ask Spirit how you can give more love to yourself.

Lavender Order

Like Jesus, Buddha, and Zoroaster, many of you have experienced the Dark Night of Soul. I compare it to the forty days and forty nights Jesus walked through the desert, purging himself of unnecessary impurities of the mind. Some of you have experienced death in the family and what comes with it. Life is not without its personal struggles. Transcending your pain and seeing the love within it will lead you into the first stages of Universal Soul Movement. Ask yourself, "What assistance can I give to Sugmad and the Sehaji Masters?" Healers who comes to heal the universe can, in time, become members of the Lavender Robe Order. This is dependent on their ability to maintain the attitude of unconditional love, the virtue of patience, listening to the heartstrings of others, and remembering that there will always be a need for compassion in this world.

The Future of this Planet

Within the contents of your heart is the future of our planet. It is the love and hope you and I share with others that makes our humanity unique and very special. What we leave behind for the future generations of the 21st Century will help humanity with its understanding of plagues, famines, and wars. The Eastern Nations, to include Africa and its renaissance, will reap prosperity and economic wealth, while the North American and Western Powers are slated for decline. The Winds of Change are slowly beginning to reorganize our planet's world governments and countries. We must maintain a steady course of learning from those who are less fortunate and exercise the wisdom we have gained from the lessons of history. Love and the God-given need for mutual cooperation will bring yet another beautiful horizon for mankind. God must give equally to all Its children, and each continent must have their day in the sun.

A Contemplative Exercise to Develop and Improve your Dialogue with the Masters

1. Sing *"HU"* five times and allow quietude to ensue.

2. See yourself sitting with the Living Sehaji Master, or any Master you a have high regard for, under a banyan tree with a beautiful flowing stream.

3. Inwardly look into his or her eyes and begin to speak about any subject you choose.

4. Imagine a golden river moving from the Master's heart to yours. For ten to fifteen minutes listen to and reflect on the subtlety of the heart's language. Remember the

voice of the heart is softer than that of the mind.

5. Slowly open your eyes. Stay quiet, if possible, for another five minutes and let the heart keep speaking to you.

6. End the exercise with, *"Blessed Be."*

Sunday Morning Session, August 14, 2005

The Sehaji in the Court of Sat Nam

It is with great sadness that this is a "good-bye" for now, until we see each other again. Let's dispense with the physical notions of the mind's limitations. I am always with you, and this is simply the flow of the Light and Sound of God. The Way of Truth is breaking new spiritual ground and stands at the forefront of world change. The City of Ekere Tere is now fully established and underway. The wormhole within its city walls will take the participant to the City of Arhirit on the Etheric Plane and straight into the Court of Sat Nam. Though Arhirit is a wondrous city, the Court of Sat Nam is a sight to behold as well. The Court of Sat Nam is the hub where the spiritual and physical universes meet and is also where the multitude of Spiritual Masters discuss the vastness of universal knowledge. Though Kal Niranjan cannot leave his domain and walk the hallways of the Court, he sends his emissaries to gather, collect, and share knowledge with teachers of the Higher Worlds. The contingencies of Free Will keep these emissaries in continual communication with teachers residing in the God Worlds. Free Will is what makes knowledge in the Lower Worlds relative to the moment and is in constant flux.

Sat Nam is considered the first manifestation of God because he is the first God-like being of this magnitude souls see when entering the God Worlds and the last guardian of the Lower Worlds. He stands like the symbol of justice, holding in both hands that which is fair, equal and in balance with the interests of all concerned. For soul to enter through the Fifth Plane's gates means there is a shift from the self to the unitary awareness conveying the vibration of allness. Sat Nam, as a universal being, resides in this same vibration of "allness." He does not concretize a form for himself unless he needs to communicate with the Sehaji Masters. In this capacity of "allness," Sat Nam is privy to every thought, action, contingency, intention, and consequence related to the exercise of physical life. He confers to the Lords of Karma the responsibility of calculating consequences of actions in the Lower Worlds. Though Sat Nam is their Overlord, he allows the Lords of Karma to mete out justice where and as they deem fit and fair.

In The Way of Truth books to come, there will be exercises given for parents to get an understanding of their children's Soul Contracts. Babaji, the great Indian mystic, and one of my tutors, has dialogued extensively on how parenting skills naturally merge with spiritual mentoring. Spirituality can be taught to our children through heart-to-heart transmission. This perspective comes from the book soon to be released entitled, *Babaji, The Beginning Has No End*. Universally, we are all parents to the children of this Earth, but in this human theatre those who are individually given to us in life have a more important karmic relationship.

A Simple Contemplative Exercise for You to Assist Your Children's Spiritual Growth

1. As a parent, you can either sit with your children in contemplation (if possible) or you can allow extremely active children to play in the environment where you are contemplating. They will connect with you through the heart. If there are any negative engrams, this exercise will give you the insight on what to do.

2. See yourself and your child(ren) in the golden light of your selfless beingness.

3. Fill your heart with the knowingness of having Sugmad's love.

4. Once you feel the warmth of this imagery, sing *"HU"* five times, and allow five minutes of quiet to ensue.

5. Ask the Inner Master to SEE inside your child's heart.

6. After a few minutes of SILENCE, ask, *"What can I do to keep my child's heart pure?"* Trust the Inner nudges you get, and remember, any postulate you receive has the capability to dispel negative thought forms seeking to attach themselves to your children's magnetic resonance or to your home.

7. A postulate you may use is, *"I declare my home sacred, holy, and clear of all interference."* Thereafter, sing *"HU"* five times and go about your day.

8. End the exercise with, *"Blessed Be."*

There will be additional spiritual instruction relating to family in future books, discourses and spiritual manuals of The Way of Truth.

The Court of Sat Nam

Reaching the Court of Sat Nam symbolizes the loosening of the family's karma and its influence on the God seeker. It is where you as soul witness St. Germaine, Gabriel, the Grand Council, Kusulu, and Kata Daki conduct the ongoing business of the universe's operations. The Angelic Orders report to Kal Niranjan, who sends his emissaries to report to Sat Nam. The spiritual student must understand that Kal is neither good nor bad; he merely balances both polarities from the Physical to the Etheric Plane. Kal also has an

Emotional and Mental Body, but they are not constructed like our Soul Body. St. Germaine and Gabriel oversee the management and regulation of love's vibration, and so all the Angelic Orders report to them. They have oversight of the various religions, earthly spiritual orders, educational institutions, charities, and other worthwhile pursuits in this direction. They even keep the myth of Santa Claus alive and see that miracles continue to keep belief and faith in God vibrant. In the Lower Worlds, communication lines between the hierarchies is via telepathic and heart-to-heart transmission. The contingencies of humanity's Free Will keep them in continual dialogue over the alignment and realignment of creative energies.

Some participants will have the opportunity to converse with Kusulu and Kata Daki. Some have already and continue to be tutored by them. Kusulu is readily approachable in the Court and often is the initiator of conversations. He is highly revered for his wisdom, and I am supported by his counsel and far-reaching insights. Kusulu allowed me and other Sehaji to arrive safely in Africa to give my talk on its shores. I am also in the constant company of Agnotti, Milati, and Kadmon. These Masters are accessible to the participants of The Way of Truth. Their names are mantrically powered and can be used in your contemplative exercises to initiate counsel with them. To be in the presence of these Masters is unbelievable, beyond the ken of anything you could imagine. *The Book of Emergence,* (to be republished soon), is your gateway into the Court of Sat Nam and is part of your training for Sehaji Mastership. The neophyte Sehaji is the spiritual student of the Eighth and Ninth Circles, whose unfoldment in these realms includes comprehending the Aloneness and Beingness of the Void. The various realms in the God Worlds are populated by Masters who work in universal cooperation. They work from the highest aspect of love. When Milarepa confers with Sat Nam, you never suspect any feeling of superiority emanating from the Head of the Grand Council. Each being has the utmost regard for the other, and there is only respect and love emanating from their words. When teachers residing in the God Worlds find themselves with tasks taking them into the Physical Worlds, their Emotional and Mental Bodies serve as communication devices, rather than devices of the ego. The great Tibetan teacher (Rebazar Tarz) once said to Paulji that the spiritual journey actually begins on the Soul Plane, the Door of Transformation, giving us one foot in Heaven and one foot in the physical universe. Those who reside on this plane of consciousness are called "Dwellers of the Threshold."

What causes difficulty for the God seeker is their unwillingness to let go of their self-limitations, lower self tendencies, traditions, and reactions. The inhabitants of the Fifth Plane have to look at themselves like the sailors who searched for the New World and had to confront their longstanding fears. You have to plunge forward like Christopher Columbus and go over the next horizon to see what is waiting for you to experience. It is a matter of you stabilizing yourself in the God Worlds. Our Inner awareness and worlds can be like the waters of tranquility in the midst of turbulence and chaos around us. Sat Nam and his Court have been working very hard to insure that the participants of The Way of Truth learn to stabilize their consciousness to their new initiations and understand how resistance to the ways of Spirit can spiral the God seeker back into the Lower Worlds.

The Lords of Karma want you to become more focused on the re-writing of your Soul Contract. This is a part of your letting go of karma. What happens is, once you start moving from one aspect of yourself you no longer need, a domino effect ensues, and each item becomes lighter and easier to move. You must join in a greater partnership with the Sehaji who are helping you. Once responsibility is fully established in all your areas of soul creativity, life begins to shift energetically on your behalf. This is the nature of self-forgiveness. Most seekers without the spiritual training give the responsibility of their lives to an Oversoul, a guardian angel or teacher. They are fearful of the freedom that comes with their choices. The Lords of Karma will begin to relinquish their hold on the participant's destiny in proportionate degrees of their acceptance of responsibility and Mastership.

The Spiritual Master Kata Daki

When Kata reached her fifth initiation, her father thought she would be married, despite his recognition of her potential spiritual greatness. Her father was a great warrior and feared he would be killed in battle and leave Kata vulnerable to the spoils of war. After her Fifth Initiation,

Kata experienced a profound pull toward the Higher Worlds. She felt compelled to move forward in consciousness and not to look back. Her teacher at that time, Sri Gautako, assisted the development of her warrior skills to the point where she could defeat her opponent with a touch or glance. Kata will be the Spiritual Master standing next to the female Master who follows me in years to come. Many female Masters of old, like Vasitreyas, will step forward to help her in mastership. Kata's greatest area of spiritual concern is the discrimination between human and divine love. Her philosophy in this area is forthcoming in next year's discourse series. The Fifth Circle comes with blessings conferred on the family. The dwellers of the Fifth Circle can establish their family members in the Court of Sat Nam, if consent is given and if they adhere to three spiritual laws: balance, non-judgment, and unconditional love. It goes without saying that some will resist this gift of love due to fear, but this may be well and good and consistent with their Soul Contracts. Love cannot be properly received without an open heart.

The White Robe Tradition

The Master Yun See is known amongst the Sehaji for the wisdom he has shared with the students of the Light and Sound. He has been an ambassador among the various robed traditions, and all those who come into his presence benefit from his great wisdom. Yun See has opened himself to those participants who seek to be of service. He is prepared to assist and mentor those whose hearts are open to the ways of Spirit. He makes one request: "Bring only your heart." You may contact him through the use of his name as your spiritual word in your contemplative exercise.

I would like to conclude my talk with a spiritual exercise. If you would like to visit with the Masters of Sat Nam's Court, this is an exercise that will open your consciousness to what they want to share with you.

A Contemplative Exercise to Open Your Consciousness to the Masters of Sat Nam's Court

These are the steps to the contemplative exercise:

1. Sing the name of Spiritual Master *"Dan Rin"* five times.

2. Sing *"HU"* five times.

3. Allow your attention to drift to the Inner screen of the mind. Begin to visualize what the Court would look like to you.

4. Ask to be shown any information necessary for your spiritual growth. Be prepared to meet with a member of the Court and be escorted on to its grounds.

5. Stay in contemplation for at least twenty minutes.

6. End the exercise with, *"Blessed Be."*

Do not be disappointed if your visual or auditory experience is less than vivid. Know that you are having the experience because the Sehaji Masters are committed to your growth and to you becoming a member of their ranks. Thank you for your love, support, and commitment to Best-Laid Plans. I will meet you in your dreams tonight.

~ Sri Michael

Module Two:

2006 Sehaji Transcripts

"Living from the Heart"

The Way of Truth Universal Retreat

Atlanta, Georgia

April 13, 2006

Guardians of the Gates of Heaven

Milarepa, Head of the Grand Council wanted The Way of Truth to call the year 2006 "The Year of the Spiritual Warrior." Our blessed path had its official beginnings in October, 2004, and by the end of October, 2005 we were 400-strong worldwide and growing exponentially each day. Each and every member who has joined thus far is a warrior of a spiritual nature. They are strong in character and their spiritual quest is for God- Realization.

God-Realization is for the spiritually strong in nature and only those of the warrior spirit can reach the heights of the spiritual knowledge and wisdom in the God Worlds. It is the warrior's nature to seek realms beyond what is considered normal and mainstream. The high ground is a road less traveled.

The Way of Truth is based on new spiritual horizons and we are a mystery school. Many Masters of the past are speaking to each of us, giving us guidance and knowledge to reach spiritual heights we could never imagine spiritually while being still here on Earth.

Miracles are being reported every day, of events happening in participant's lives as they open their hearts to God (also known as Sugmad) and to what It wants to share with them. Through the words of Babaji, Milarepa, Jesus and the vanguard of female masters such as Lemlet, Senna, and Mary Magdalene, relationships are being healed, long standing health issues are turning for the Good, and loved ones who have passed on have reappeared and spoken at length with those they have left on Earth. Artistic talents are growing in leaps and bounds, and personalities are being refined and becoming more loving. The lists of stories and of lives changing for the Good are endless. When our website is fully updated some of those stories will be available for your reading. The grounds of our mystery school are dynamic and deeply penetrating. The spiritual warrior has given Love in the face of daily challenges and to the sleep state of slumbering souls who cannot discriminate between fear and love, or judgment and Divine Free Will. Give only Love. This is what makes the true spiritual warrior. See life for what it really is - a training ground for soul development. Forge forward and do not look back at your past hurts.

It is "Living from the Heart" that insures our spiritual freedom; open your heart for true healing, greater possibilities in life, greater love, and greater creativity in all aspects of life.

Living in your heart is being the Spiritual Warrior. The mind is often of little use when one is living in the ways of Spirit. The heart center is the communication center of this universe and the next. Ask Sugmad and the Inner Master to fill your heart each morning with Light and Sound, with love, joy, understanding, healing, and guidance in word and deed, and see what happens. You will feel your Being, your very Soul filling up with the abundance of happiness and well being.

By becoming a spiritual warrior and living from the heart your life will unfold into the passage of beautiful pages of love, joy, and peace.

The Grand Council chose the theme of "Living from the Heart" to open our hearts to a deeper meaning of love and what it is to convene with God within ourselves. To live from the Heart one needs to look and listen to the great and small matters of life in equal proportions. In nature, from those who are Spirit's subtle channels of Light and Sound to the birds that bring messages of love and warning, communications from the Heart are different from communications from the mind. When we learn to listen and speak from the Heart we hear much more and we give much more. True listening is heart-filled. If someone tells you they are suffering, listening with your mind often compounds and intensifies their discomfort. You will not respond to them in a way that will be of any comfort. When listening with your Heart you are more in tune with their consciousness, and you will respond in a kinder, gentler tone.

Living from the Heart is drinking from the pure waters of the Sea of Love and Mercy. The good, bad and indifferent are all Its Creations in place here for us to make our choices each and every day as to how we should manifest and create. Every choice we make has a cause, a root-cause, and an effect. Root causes are events of past lives we have agreed to bring contractually into our present life. Cause and effect often operates like a mathematical equation in Algebra, with known and unknown variables; and works exponentially in connective sequence to people, events, and objects in our personal environments. To live from the Heart in God Consciousness is a learning process that multiplies upon itself like fire to the second power; fire to the third power; and fourth into Infinity. Start each day asking Sugmad and the Inner Master to fill you with the Light and Sound of the Universe. Thank them for leading you in serving the best interests of all concerned as you go through your day. Sing the HU Song at every opportunity; stay in vigilant practice of your daily contemplative exercises, and what you want to move and change in your life will move in accordance with your state of consciousness to receive the gifts of Spirit.

Living from the Heart makes us simply more appealing people and human beings. We laugh more, smile more, and loved ones, friends, and family are drawn to us because of the Light coming from us. When living from the Heart in

God Consciousness, your spiritual vibrations become more expansive and you become more aware of what you say to others and what actions you take.

Living from the Heart in God Consciousness is to love all life, and all things. Sometimes in life we have to give detached goodwill and love because of the choices and judgments of others. We are all here for lessons; and we must be forgiving of the shortcomings of others, so making the proper choices in this life either heightens or lowers the soul's vibratory awareness.

Living from the Heart in God Consciousness means reaching deep into the Heart and knowing that a mind that is not in servitude will confound and confuse you. Feel the blissful love radiating between you, the Inner Master, and Sugmad. Be the love you seek; keep your heart pure and be kind in your countenance and words. Give acknowledgement to the lonely in heart; rejoice in Africa's Emerging Renaissance; be ever vigilant in the giving of appreciation and gratitude for the nectar of Sugmad's love permeating the very air we breathe. Soul is eternal and this life is only one phase of its growth here on Earth. Though painful at times, all that we are and can be is founded and exists upon this one, great universal love that is living and existing from the Heart.

Living from the Heart uplifts the home's vibration for Life's opportunities of economic growth and understanding to occur. The home is the heart and sanctuary for those who reside there. Spiritual comfort, beauty, health, organization, and happiness are all reflected in the home. Living from the Heart raises the conscious choices of those residing in the home.

When we consciously see with Soul's Eyes what the heart consciousness does for our home, thought patterns and nutritional regiments change; families become more health conscious. They begin to cognize; to realize each source of food on this planet holds a vibration that either gives energy or takes it away. To test the sanctity of the food eaten, ask Spirit as you purchase food if it will give you energy or take it away. Trust your nudges and intuition; they will improve in clarity and focus over time by using them. The higher vibration foods are those whose plant source is in their natural or raw state. This will give your body its purest form of vitamins and enzymes. This posture has been known to be very enhancing to our resiliency as we develop and age. We will naturally shift in our choices of food and those choices we will make unthinkingly will be comprised of the highest vibration of food available to us.

The colors of our home are also one of vibration; and must reflect the signature of your spiritual vibration. Often when we choose colors we like, they are generally reflective of this perspective. Staying in the heart will lead you to the colors that reflect the highest aspects of your consciousness. Everything in life is energy and holds and reflects color and everything we choose to place in our home holds different frequencies and amounts of energy. One way to spiritually get in tune with the beautification of your home is to ask Spirit to reflect your heart consciousness with what you want to bring in your home. Then sing HU three times and trust yourself and Spirit.

Living from the Heart and this quest will bring more cohesiveness to your relationships with loved ones in the home. The lines of communication become stronger over time and the Heart will teach you to make better choices in the words you use. In a gist, your verbal word inventory will change. Some words have the capability to recharge forgotten memories that do not have any relation to the present. Heart Consciousness guides us in letting go of words that are obsolete and no longer a part of our spiritual environment. This expansion of conscious communication is a progressive pattern. If you are living by yourself, living from the Heart means to love yourself, all that you are, and all that you are becoming as a God-Realized being. This actually applies to each individual, whether you live alone or with others. Seek the Love of Sugmad and the guidance of the Inner Master each day by asking for the Light and Sound and love of the universe to fill you with Its abundance. Choices of the Heart are guided by Sugmad and exceed the limitations of the mind.

By progressing in Heart, in God Consciousness, and in living from the Heart many newfound opportunities will come to you. The Universe is full of wonder, gifts of love, light, sound, creativity, peace, health, personal fulfillment, joy, and so much more.

Our Social Lives

Socially, living from the Heart naturally repels those who bring with them negativity and vibrations not compatible with our present state of consciousness, and attracts those who will lift us up. Everyone has areas in their lives that need attention. The Lower Worlds are in constant flux and change.

Living from the Heart socially is a key factor to having true support from our friends, who are like angels on Earth to add to our lives each and every day.

When we learn to live from the Heart, many people will be naturally attracted to us because we will be vibrating at such a level of beauty that loved ones and friends will want to share in the beautiful glow emanating from within.

Friendship is that of helping, uplifting, caring, and bringing meaning and value into a person's life. It is also a "looking in" with the Heart and realizing even good people have faults. We all fall short in some area. The good our friends put out in the world far outweighs their pitfalls and shortcomings. Friendships end when the Heart is no longer open to the other person's needs, emotions, values, personal beliefs, and freedom of expression. We are all growing at different rates and in different areas. Living from the Heart will let you know we are all vulnerable to mistakes and know each of you is learning along The Way of Truth. It is having a forgiving heart towards transgressions from the past when friends fail our expectations, and also forgiving yourself. Forgiveness conserves the energy of the righteous. The spiritual practice of forgiving is an integral part of our growth towards being God-Realized and Living from the Heart. With loving effort certain misunderstandings can be realized, and love can again bloom and grow. Our universe is one beautiful garden waiting for the seeds of love you can plant. Just the giving of love is the key to personal happiness; find this place within yourself before you search to conjoin this emotion with another. Being your own anchor brings more balance, confidence, and stability to any human relationship.

Milarepa

Feel the love and joy of Sugmad, the Grand Council, and the Silent Nine. It is your right as soul to ask for the best life has to offer. The God-Power within us partners itself with the flow and guidance of Spirit.

As friendships go, we all need them for support and love. This universe operates on the foundation of mutual cooperation and goodwill. Friends bring ideas, support, and new areas of motivation into our lives. We can laugh, we can cry with our closest and oldest of friends; they become family, and some are family of olde. Lift up your friends, new and old. Compliment them for the good works they do, their ideas, talents, and skills. Let them know you love them; don't be afraid to say so.

Work Environment

Living from the Heart in the workplace is often giving love in a "detached manner." Not everyone in your work environment will be someone you will want to be close with. Our coworkers come with lessons to learn. Allow no word to escape from your mouth that does not emanate from your Heart. Detached goodwill means giving them respect, goodwill, and recognition of them as soul, with the right of spiritual freedom and expression. The Heart Consciousness will neutralize the jealousness and envy of others. I would do five silent HUs in my work environment and then speak inwardly in my Middle Eye to anyone who is giving me challenges.

Saturday Night Session

Salutations and Acknowledgements

This afternoon I have incorporated into my talk a power point presentation of Ekere Tere, City of Light, and pictures of the female spiritual masters who have come forth to work with you and me in the completion of Best-Laid Plans of the Grand Council, the Silent Nine, and Sugmad. The books

Ekere Tere, City of Light and *Guardians of the Gates of Heaven* have been completed for release before the end of this year. *Guardians of the Gates* will feature the female masters you will see tonight. Also it gives me great joy to share with you the release of The Way of Truth book *Babaji, the Beginning Has No End*, and our Holy Book *The Way of Truth Eternal – Book I* will be available before the end of this month. *Book II* is forthcoming in 2008.

(Slide show begins.)

The Consciousness of the Heart Determines Soul's Entry

The Heart is the ground switch for the transmission of Soul's message to its physical counterpart. The wider and more expansive the heart opening is, the greater the clarity soul's daily communication with us has.

Ekere Tere – Vortex Open

A great many of our participants have viewed their entry into the classrooms in Ekere Tere from this angle. Placing this picture in your Third Eye gives great comfort and has been the stimulus for Soul Journeys into the city.

Ekere Tere – The Main Entrance

The architects were the Kerminites who built Agam Des. The purpose of Ekere Tere was to assist in Africa's Renaissance, to take some of the workload of various teachers in Agam Des, to teach higher techniques of living and creative manifestation to the participants of the Light and Sound. The list of Soul Journeyers entails an extensive array of clergy from all walks of life. It has helped me in my restriction of black magic in Africa.

Up-close View of Main Entrance

(No comments made here.)

Main Entrance Gate /The Holy Fire of HU

There are simply no words that can capture the beauty and essence of beingness of the HU; it is Sugmad's life-code.

Door Opening to Ekere Tere

Children are also being tutored in the classes. Some of you will see beautiful transformations in your own children and our youth of the Light and Sound.

Layout of Ekere Tere

This is my preferred angle of entry into the City of Light.

Library – Core Chamber Floor

Many of the spiritual masters like Sri Leytor, Kusulu, Rumi and many members of the Grey, White and Lavender Robes gather research in the library and also confer with the artisans, poets, musicians, and academic teachers under their mentorship here. It is not unusual to see Kata Daki speaking with a representative of Sat Nam, Kal Niranjan, and the Lords of Karma here.

Soul's Purification and Education

(No comments here.)

Spiritual Signature of Sehaji Mastership

All of the Sehaji Hierarchies have agreed to use this symbol and much will be elaborated on about the Symbol in our next Holy Book which is already in progress.

Ursula Pendragon – My Lady of the Lake

A glimpse of this Female Sehaji Master is in *The Guardians of the Gates* book. A book manifesting called *Pendragon* will speak of the ancient Druid mysteries around King Arthur and Merlin. Ursula states Arthur existed in the time frame of approximately 400-500 A.D. Oral tradition was the basis of Druid tradition and very little existed after Rome waged its war against this culture. During certain periods of this planet's evolution, it was possible to walk into areas of the High Astral Planes.

Lemlet – Seer of Prophecy

This great avatar has been a liaison in my communications between The White and Grey Robe Traditions. Lemlet's life is a portrait of courage and determination. Against incredible odds, personal loss and physical limitations;

Lemlet gained spiritual mastership while taking the role of a medicine women (shaman.) She experienced a near detrimental fall down a mountainside which left her permanently disabled for the rest of her life. She experienced the loss of her entire family during a longstanding tribal war. She was taken in by the conquering tribe for her gifts of prophecy and medicine. Lemlet touched everyone who was in her physical environment with unspeakable bliss and Sugmad's Love. She offers the participant her skills of prophecy in Ekere Tere.

Arutu - Sehaji in Africa's Renaissance

This spiritual master is working with our brothers and sisters of the Light and Sound in Africa. She works at the right hand of Towart Managi and like Rebazar Tarz, physically manifests herself to be of direct assistance to participants there. She has saved the lives of several participants while they were engaged in a physical struggle against black magicians. Arutu will be offering classes on how the participant can find the right counterpart.

Kata Daki - Spiritual Warrior and Master

Kata learned the art of martial arts, weaponry, and horsemanship amongst the far reaching nomadic tribes of Asia. No man has ever rivaled her in "hand to hand" combat. She was forced to learn the art of self-defense due to the male chauvinism of the times. It is Kata's mission to further the spiritual skills (life skills) of participants.

Mentorship with her would also entail how to carry the God Force in non-power and without ego. Kata is concerned with the participant's inability to use their initiation beyond the Seventh Circle properly. She was one of the masters who stood constantly by my side when the spiritual manuals were written, to guide our participants inwardly in the creative skills of their Circles.

Prisca and the Early Roman Christian Community

Prisca's Favorite Prayer for Facing Life Trials:

> *Come into my Heart, my Lord*
> *I pray to you each day*
> *Show me how to live my life*
> *While walking in Your Way*
>
> *Help me to be willing*
> *To do all that you may ask*
> *Guide me to your Heart within*
> *From there I do each task*
>
> *Protect me from the dangers*
> *Lying in my mind and out*
> *Show me how to surrender*
> *All my fears and doubts*

Lead me to let go
Of things that are not mine
And live forever in your joy
I will be forever Thine.

Read the above prayer, sing five *"HU's"* thereafter, and begin your day.

Prisca was from an affluent family of Rome who gained spiritual mastership during the Christian Apostolic Community under Paul. She was a major architect in keeping Christian secret communications intact and the scheduling of services and meetings in the catacombs. Communication amongst the community was not possible without Prisca. She is presently working with the Church fathers, ministry, and monastic orders. Many Catholic fathers are in direct communication with her and attend her classes in Ekere Tere.

Vasitraya

She greets you with a wave of HU and says "Sugmad is my Sword and the Living Master is my Shield." This is not her birth name in the time she gained mastership. This name was given to her to safeguard the origins of her British ancestry and family who are still in England and India. Her name was conferred by Kata Daki. She was fluent in four to five Middle Eastern and Asian languages. She was mentored primarily by Kata Daki; it is her viewpoint that women of today must have the skills of a warrior as much as ever if they want to discover and achieve their missions in life. She is mentoring a great many female participants in dealing with chauvinism in the work and family environment, and some are in direct conversation with her right now. She has been focusing on the development of spiritual insights into choosing the right occupation, work environments and partners in life.

Senna – Metaphysics and Approaching the Abyss

One of Senna's earliest teachers was Parimenides and she took an early and serious interest in Philosophy and Metaphysics. It is Senna's view that metaphysics explains the nature of beingness and its origin, the fundamental causes of life, creation itself and the structures of the worlds, as we know them, or come to know them. Metaphysics was her spiritual springboard into the God Worlds. She believes God calls upon all souls to activate their God-given powers of creativity, the power of Universal Soul Movement into worlds unseen, and the freedom to choose and use discrimination in order to continue with the work of creation. Senna considers "fear of the unknown" the major deterrent of the participant in gaining the Eighth Circle of Consciousness. Love is the antidote to fear. The Aloneness one feels in this Circle and above is a reflection of what it is to be Sugmad, to be one's own reference point of conscious creativity. The mind and its consciousness have no grounding here in these realms. It is this fear that stimulates the ego. She wanted to remind all of our participants the initiations are not badges of pride. If the participant breaks the Law of Silence regarding their initiation and spiritual development, their Inner mentoring and soul movement will be halted until they learn humility, love, and service to the universe.

Brigit of the Picts, Scotland

Brigit will be dialoguing with her students about the ancient Druid mysteries and the secrets around the building of Stonehenge and other architectural stone marvels through Ireland, England, and Scotland. Brigit discusses the relationship between the inhabitants of Atlantis and Lemurians and ancient stone structures of Egypt, Mexico, South America, and Asia. She also discusses the "goddess traditions" of olden times, when the Earth was very young. She will mentor only those who are firmly grounded in the Light and Sound without ego and self-interest. Ursula Pendragon and Kata Daki were her primary mentors before reaching the outer rung of God-Realization. She will present a technique for seeing into one's Life Contract and the development of prophetic vision in the *Guardians* book.

Mary Magdalene - Beloved of Jesus

Mary said that no one could stand around Jesus and not feel the tremendous love of God. She said he was everything to her. Jesus was so beautiful, so loving, so gentle, and magnificent. She often felt like a moth flying too close to the flame. Mary states when she first looked into his eyes, she was transported into Heaven. A chorus of angels sang so sweetly, as all of time and earthly existence seemed suspended in a halo of golden light. Jesus was one of first men of that day who spoke of women's rights and their equality.

Mother Mary

Both Mary's will speak about their travel to France under the protection of Joseph of Arimathea. Mother Mary will also talk about the Grail Stone, its secret use, and what Jesus' teacher Zadok wanted him to use it for. The Grail Stone has the power of creative manifestation spoken about in the *Ekere Tere, City of Light* book. Mary will elaborate on why the Grail Stone and the Cup of Christ were separated and what countries they are presently in. The Grail Stone and Cup have the power to restore the Middle East back into its former peace and balance as it was in the year 850. Mary said her son taught her to be a vessel of God's love, to be a living vehicle for the love, word and actions of God, to surrender the ego and treat others with dignity, respect, and unconditional love, and to give without judgment and give reverence to the belief of others, and other ways of life.

Mary concludes her chapter with her memories of the crucifixion and what happened to the Spear of Longinas (the spear possessed by the Centurion whose spear pierced Jesus' body.) It became a spiritual talisman of great power and gave world leadership to those who possessed it throughout time.

Jesus of Nazareth

Jesus wanted to render closure to Volume One of *Guardians of the Gates of Heaven*. It was his way of being in unity of consciousness with his beloved Mary's. Jesus sees each living being, including animals and beings from other lands, worthy of great respect and unconditional love. Jesus says the female God seekers are the unsung heroes; they show and demonstrate how one person can make a difference in the workplace, home, and environment. They show how the love of Sugmad can bridge the singularity of the individual with the quantum-universal foundation of God-Realization. Walk this life filled with love, for it permeates the air and brings out the infinite beauty of Living from the Heart. Beauty creates peace. Peace radiates, restores, and replenishes. The female Sehaji are here to teach the lessons of humility, fortitude, and courage. The female masters have stationed themselves so anyone can access their love, wisdom and tutelage through the spiritual techniques throughout the book, *Guardians*. Jesus will play an instrumental role with Archangel Gabriel in the completion of the two books, *Mohammed, Man of God, Brother of Jesus* and *Revelations*. They have been slated for release in 2007 along with the book, *Discovery of Self*.

Archangel Gabriel, Head of All Angelic Orders

Gabriel gives an extensive message in his chapter in the book, *Ekere Tere*. Gabriel has been a spiritual mentor to countless Spiritual Teachers such as Babaji, Jesus, Mohammed, Zoroaster, and Buddha, to include a few. He also oversees the healing orders like the Brown Robes and the White Brotherhood, and assists in the work of today's natural medicine. He has been a liaison between Kal Niranjan, the Lords of Karma, Sat Nam, the Grand Council, and the Living Master.

As Head of All Angelic Orders, he oversees the missions of Archangels Michael, Alexander, the two Mary's, and Althea in *Guardians of the Gates*; their work will be elaborated on later. His work has been invaluable to the Sehaji White Robe Hierarchy. Their combined spiritual work has kept thus far some countries falling into revolution and chaos. The decisions of present leaders around the world are opening themselves to radical change if they do not return relics they have appropriated without consent to their countries of origin. Gabriel and Yaubl Sacabi will explain why this is coming to a climatic fork in the road in *The Dialogues of Yaubl Sacabi*.

Gabriel says the Father of All has placed much responsibility on the shoulders of the various teachers and The Way of Truth participants. Each of you will be a channel of love for the continuation and balance of this planet. Father cherishes each of you as Its children of Light and Sound, and Guardians of the Gates of Heaven. Each of you will be "heart-to-heart" guided to your life-mission. See the love in ALL for nothing else exists but the love our Father has given us. Father sees in each of you the promise of greater balance, and more love and more compassion that each of you will bring to humanity. Call upon me (Dan Rin) when the need prevails.

(End of PowerPoint presentation.)

(Sri Michael's talk continues)

St. Germaine

He often works on independent projects and was a spiritual advisor to the Knights Templars from their inception to their spiritual peak.

Souls come in all forms from all Planes

As in Agam Des, Ekere Tere is a City that accommodates visitors of the Light and Sound from distant places. We seem as different to them as they do to us. Some have the ability to alter the way the mind is filtering their appearances.

Nine Star Tetrahedron

In the universes of commanders of the Light and Sound, such as Kadmon and Agnotti, the Cycle of Threes has embedded in kinetic energy, in other words built-in movement. Three dimensional thought is the conventional, normal way to conduct life. Three dimensional objects can be mantrically developed to propel objects through space. It actually folds space and time when the conscious state is awake and in full use of mental capabilities. It utilizes areas of the mental consciousness not yet developed and uncovered in the human brain. It has the ability to polarize thought forms into projective force, which has been essential to growth and evolution of races not known by humanity yet, but this day will come.

Kadmon states the ability to see the "three in three" is the secret behind all creative manifestation in the Physical Plane. Many of the participants entering into Ekere Tere are using this secret via their ability to receive the spiritual classes there. Ekere Tere is a gateway leading straight into the Heart of Sugmad; it is the "power of three" that makes this Universal Soul Movement possible. The Power of Three creates a wormhole effect.

The three is manifesting unity; it holds the universe into a cohesive whole. The three entails Sugmad creating the seed for soul's growth, Soul Consciousness' expansion from the illusionary experience, and Sugmad's expansion from soul's expanded consciousness.

The Secret of Three and Nine is key to the use of non-power, which is the efficient use of the Law of Neutrality. The use of this law means you give the detached goodwill without placing conditions upon this affection. It also means you simply recognize others as soul first, with the knowledge that what you are seeing before you is a role that soul is playing. Soul is awakening to greater concentric cycles of three; God and Its children exist in an eternal cycle of reciprocity, much like a child learning from its parent, and the parent learning from the child.

This centering of your Self, which is use of the Nine Pointed Tetrahedron, slowly releases the negative engrams from your magnetic resonance, otherwise known as *sanskaras*, an energy wrapping around your body. The *sanskaras* hold the karmic energy patterns that repetitively occur. This cleansing of the *sanskaras* opens the participants to the positive aspects of life, attracting positive events and opportunities.

A weekly contemplative technique with the Nine-Pointed Tetrahedron

1. Once a week, use the Nine-Pointed Tetrahedron as your mantra by visualizing it in your Middle Eye and sing *"HU"* intermittently during your contemplation. There is no set frequency of times to use the holy word HU.

2. Allow Soul to lead you in the exercise and be attentive to the vibration resonating inside of you.

3. Do not exceed the use of this exercise more than the allotted time, you could run into "spiritual indigestion" and you will not be allowed to use everything you are receiving.

4. End the exercise with, *"Blessed Be."*

Nine-pointed tetrahedron of The Way of Truth

A Tetrahedron Exercise Utilizing Milarepa's Devotion Prayer

I would like to invite you into doing a short exercise involving the tetrahedron.

1. Close your eyes and let's visualize the tetrahedron in our "Middle Eye" for one minute.

2. Let us now sing *"HU"* for an approximate minute and I will then read "Milarepa's Devotion Prayer" and then I will say "open your eyes slowly." (For prayer, see Ivory Coast, 2006 Retreat, under the section entitled "Mohammed, Man of God, Brother of Jesus.")

The Law of Opposites

The Teacher Kadmon wanted me to briefly go over this law with you. It entails how life often presents you with what you are trying to avoid. There are challenges that will come up in our life and most of the time we are all guilty of putting them off until we cannot any longer. Approach each challenge with the attitude that there is something in this event you can simply learn from and grow from. Most, if not all times, the problem changes. It changes because we have changed; our problem is nothing without us; we give our challenges and problems meaning. They exist because of our consciousness. Choose where you want to go in consciousness.

Most of our problems in life are created by us living in our mind rather than living from our heart. If we were to start each day by asking God and the Inner Master, Dan Rin, to fill us with love, Light and Healing Power from the top of our heads to the bottom of our toes, and bless every word and deed, we would see the glory of Heaven that comes to us each day and we would not enact deeds that were not savory unto ourselves or our fellow man. Living from the heart is something we have to practice each and every day. This life is full of temptation, egoistic, and selfish acts. We are constantly bombarded with the toys of the mind. If we live in the heart we can control the temptation of living in the mind and walk the footsteps of the Earth's savants and saints.

Madame Blavatsky of the Theosophical Society

She has conveyed to me that each of you is carrying the message of God back to your home. It will take the form of love, balance, peace, and understanding because each of you are stepping into the higher aspects of living from the Heart, and as the universe moves to its next level of conscious evolution with us, the love and wisdom that expands from our hearts will have an unimaginable domino effect upon our environments. Give Love to each challenge; give detached goodwill to those who presents those challenges. The love, truth, and wisdom developed in our collective hearts will bring a greater vibration of knowledge and fiber to The Way of Truth. We are the conduits, that is, the channels for a universal purification of all paths and walks of life.

Law of Love

The teacher Kadmon wanted to convey to each of you that it is love and love alone which is the binding force of God's universe of multidimensional reality. It is love that it is the glue that keeps souls interacting, and unified in purpose. Love creates, gestates, and births life on all dimensions of reality. The most obvious of love's presence is the bonding of man and woman. Without love, all animal and plant life would die. Love is interwoven into the Law of Three, the Law of the Trinity. Love requires the marriage of opposing and neutral forces; it requires rhythm, energy, motion, and multiplicity. This facilitates growth and expansion into greater areas of expression and service. The love of God, love of self, and love of others are being expressed by each of you and this alone places you at the Gates of Heaven because you are living from the heart. When you are low in spirit, the African master of olde would say "My strength grows directly from God's Love, Will and Compassion." then HU in three cycles of three.

Blessed Be.

~ Sri Michael

The Way of Truth Universal Retreat

Ivory Coast

August 12, 2006

Morning Salutations

It is with privilege and honor that I welcome each of you to the Ivory Coast Universal Seminar Retreat. Milarepa, Head of the Grand Council wanted The Way of Truth to call the year 2006 "The Year of The Spiritual Warrior." Our blessed path had its official beginnings in October, 2004 and by the end of October, 2005 we became an exponentially larger mystery school. It is the love in this room that is ushering forth Africa's Renaissance. The riches of the Earth, materially and spiritually, reside in Africa. What brought Europe here to your doorstep is what Africa has to offer the world. Each of you, of the warrior spirit is strong in spiritual character and your quest is God-Realization and the Best-Laid Plans of Sugmad, and the spiritual hierarchies of this universe.

The grounds and path you will walk upon will become sacred and holy; the love you carry is Sugmad's love for all life and Its grace of compassion and spiritual freedom. I thank each of you for the journey you have undertaken. I stand before you, giving gratitude and appreciation for the commitment you have made. I will now place the helm of this seminar in the capable hands of our staff. Blessed Be, Sri Michael.

Saturday Night Session

Mohammed, Man of God, Brother of Jesus

The Middle East has been the cyclic meeting place for many souls, to include you and myself, to purge the dross of unnecessary spiritual impurities. Between year 600 A.D. to 1100, the Middle East was considered a Heaven on Earth. The Middle East was reaping the benefits of the Quran and the spiritual teachings of the Holy Prophet, Mohammed. Through the Archangel Gabriel's mentoring, Mohammed stimulated humanity's achievements in medicine, academics, literature, and art. It was the esoteric nature of the Quran that inspired its believers to new heights of spiritual understanding.

Mohammed has come forth within the book *Mohammed, Man of God, Brother of Jesus* to (1) prevent world-wide mass destruction, (2) to intensify a golden age on Earth, and (3) to provide a wider base of training and awareness of the ascension process into the God Worlds. It is a time for the brothers and sisters of Abrahaim to return to the table of their father and partake of the spiritual food and love imparted by the Torah, Old & New Testaments of the Christian Bible and the Quran. Each holy text was mentored and God's holy words were given by the Archangel Gabriel to their respective messengers.

Abrahaim was chosen by God for his strong leadership skills and it was written into his Soul Contract before his birth. In historical theology, Abrahaim is the Father of Judaic and Moslem Culture and Christianity is the child of Judaism. Jesus, being of Jewish descent, was mentored by Gabriel in the same shape, manner, and form as Mohammed, with one exception - Mohammed had no need to learn the art of invisibility and creative manifestation.

Mohammed wrote the Quran's holy message as the Third Covenant for the disenfranchised children of Ishmael, Abrahaim's eldest son. The theological conflict between Judaic, Christian and Moslem has to do energetically with each group unwilling to see each other as a legitimate extension of God's message. The foundation of all three ways of life is love, compassion, and charity. Can we not open our hearts to see the love in all walks of life? Let us allow God's message to usher forth in all languages, in all tongues, and you will be a vigilant spiritual warrior in Africa's long awaited Renaissance to see this holy mission fulfilled.

Mohammed wanted to share this devotional, contemplative prayer with each of you and all peoples of the world. True healing begins within one's own heart.

Dearest Beneficent and Merciful Allah

I declare myself to be your glove
For Your wisdom, truth and love
Fill my whole body full of light,
For all are equal in your sight

May Peace be born of Moslem and Jew
May all awaken to honor You
When we embrace the brotherhood of man,
We'll meet in the heart of the Great I AM

Please remind me when my heart turns cold
That my brother's hands were made to hold
Though children of an earthy mother,
All derive from One Holy Father

No matter what time of the day
Help me always choose what to say
I give and receive love to each others fill,
I choose this moment to obey Your will.

The Question of Faith

Many God seekers of all walks of life have asked me about how we cultivate faith in God. Faith is an unquestioning reliance in a power you know will always be true. Faith has to begin with belief and learning to trust what comes to your heart. Faith is trust without reservation and I understand this is not an easy task. The cultivation of our faith comes with a willingness to surrender to God's Will instead of trying to control what you feel and would like to be the outcome of your actions. Go into contemplation, do five HUs and say, "I move as You will, heal me and lead me." A large part of faith is simply a "Letting go of."

The Question of Knowing God's Will

In the worlds of duality (our physical worlds) soul is given Its own will and the ability to learn and use it with the fullness of freedom. It is only when soul experiences the feeling of separation that it can determine if its will is in alignment and balanced with God's Will. Otherwise, soul could not determine its own individuation from that of God.

God wants only the best for Its children. I ask the question "Am I acting in the highest state of love?" and trust what my heart gives me. Love never short-changes soul, and always seems to reveal what our physical eyes do not see.

Giving Love Daily

Devote your life, in every moment to purity and faithfulness. And adhere to the Will and Laws of God. Cultivate patience, perseverance, gratitude, forgiveness, compassion, tolerance, courage, generosity, and self-control. Use your imagination and develop your thoughts in loving ways to others. Be kind and exercise spontaneous acts of joy, laughter, and humor; make your own choices and mistakes, learn and grow and feel free to forgive yourself. Find reward in the giving and do not wait for the accolades at the end of the road.

How to Find Devotion

Devotion to Its Cause is found in service, charity and the daily practice of the contemplative exercises. All three aspects open the heart, the universal transmitter of God's love, to a greater glory. With humility, comes the birthplace of compassion. Without humility, humanity thinks only of itself, and places ego above the Will of God. Mohammed sees humility like a soap the God seekers use to cleanse themselves from the daily grime of living, and wash their Inner Bodies.

What of Humility?

Humility is dwelling in one's heart. It is balanced, knowingness in the Silence, serene, peaceful, and tender, but strong in character. Humility is the entrance to Divine Love.

What is Knowledge?

Knowledge is spiritual energy flowing from Allah. Knowledge is spiritual energy flowing from Allah. The Astral, Causal, Mental, and Etheric Bodies break down the Light and Sound into spectra of frequency resonances that result in the human consciousness materializing these particles into tangible use. Physics is the intellectual portion of humanity attempting to bridge an understanding between the material and spiritual worlds. Science will be finding more answers in metaphysics and natural medicine as humanity places closure to this century.

Soul is the guardian of the lower bodies I have alluded to. There is no limitation for soul's ability to store and accumulate knowledge and its access to it is cognitively instant and intuitive.

The Spiritual Laws of God

Laws for the Universe

Spiritual Laws create the order necessary for the balance of this universe. They create lines of descending energy from God into the Universal Mind Consciousness and into collective mental consciousness of all intelligible life. These laws have an origin beyond the span of this universe and are a driver's manual for those God seekers who want to attain God-Realization in their lifetime. Without the universal Laws, which define function and form, there would be nothingness; there would be no possibility of being in the material worlds.

Spiritual Laws Supersedes Humanity's Laws

Universal laws are immutable, eternal, indisputable, vital for all life, and foundational for all existence, in all planes and spheres, planets, countries and individual souls. Universal laws supersede the laws of humanity, which exist for human beings to interact without hurting one another for all to live in harmony for the greatest good.

A Special Exercise for the Retreat

This mantra I will give you is intended to answer questions of the heart and initiate material action in the Physical World.

1. First, I want you to empty-out your mind and tell your body to rest.

2. Now let us sing *"HU"* five times and allow Spirit to place you in quietude.

3. Now repeat after me this mantra three times: *"A-TU-DAS-A-TO-TUMA," "A-TU-DAS-A-TO-TUMA," "A-TU-DAS-A-TO-TUMA."*

4. Now say what this mantra means: *"I stand in Sugmad's Supreme Consciousness."*

5. Now pose a question to your heart; soul, and Sugmad, who is in direct contact with you. You can ask to be directed and led in a certain way to fulfill a goal.

6. (Silent contemplation for about three minutes.)

7. Now, slowly open your eyes.

I do not want you to put closure on this technique. We want this high state of awareness to stay with you throughout your day and evening. If you repeat certain mantras consistently over time, they will signaturize themselves to your spiritual bodies. The vibrations of the mantra will begin to turn on automatically when you have need of them. The whole gist is to identify and acknowledge what vibrations are on. Each contemplative technique has a special frequency of the Light and Sound; once identified it can be turned on consciously. This is one step from being able to move consciousness to any plane of existence of your choosing. God Consciousness is in the "here and now."

The Law of Love

Love is the prime attribute of the Divine Being; it is the Law of Love sustaining ALL life. It is the energy that moves all subatomic cells. It is the contingencies of man's will and heart that opens and chooses to deny this wave of infinite Love ushering from Sugmad's heart.

The Law of Compassion

The Law of Compassion is the ability of Soul to see beyond the illusion of what seems to be happening, to see into the heart of Love that pours outward from Sugmad and exists in all living beings. Compassion is a demonstration of the Law of Love; it is the practice of the Divine Presence. Compassion inspires more Love and is a reflection of the Divine in you. And let us have compassion for our own imperfections. Give compassion; give mercy; give love; give to life.

The Law of Forgiveness

Sugmad knows intelligible life is prone to pitfalls, mistakes, and misleading behavior and all of this is within the scope of forgiveness. To forgive is to acknowledge the capacity of Sugmad's love for all life. It is through forgiveness that true wisdom is developed. Illusion develops when the human consciousness unfolds with the concept that it is separated and fragmented from the whole. We live, breathe, and exist within the unity of God. Contemplation and contemplative prayer synchronizes the Inner Bodies into "facsimile alignment." This is an Inner balance that facilitates an abundant flow of Light and Sound to uplift and productively change our lives.

To gain connection and wholeness, God gave us the vehicle and method of forgiveness. Forgiveness is an action; God's gift for-giving, it is a representative of God's Grace and Mercy. Love God, love one another, forgive the transgressions of others, let God (also known as Sugmad) guide your hands and return you to being in the flow and expression of God's Love and Everlasting Grace.

The Gift of Charity

The question is always posed to me, "Are we not our neighbor's keeper?" We can often lift our neighbor's heart with a kind word, a smile and a listening ear. This is love in action. Is a slice of bread much to give when we have a whole loaf? The charity I speak of is also the holding of one's tongue, seeking to understand the hearts of others, and being patient with those who test our spiritual balance. It is the Heart behind what we give of ourselves.

The Law of Silence

Sugmad's Voice is never silent, but the human consciousness must become silent in order to hear, see and be in the knowingness of Its understanding. This happens only when one is still, quiet, listening to the still Voice within and closed to the distractions of the Outer world, emotions and mental chatter. This quietude will lead to Sugmad speaking to you via intuition, visions and dreams in purity and truth. Secondly, this law teaches the discipline of understanding that what Spirit gives us - most times - is for "our ears only." Discrimination must always be used when considering the disclosure of high spiritual information to others.

Soul can tune in on Sugmad's directives by singing HU, an ancient name for God. The daily insights Spirit can give can change one's karmic balance, create a new cause, or cure an illness. To walk this path giving love to our fellow God seekers is part of our great goal of living, but to do for others what they can do for themselves often hinders their development and defeats the purpose of life's challenges. Therefore, the discriminate use of the Law of Silence is one of the greatest forms of love, just like a good parent who allows their children to learn and grow strong, so each soul is charged with the same sense of discrimination. Each of us must always find a balance in the love we give. We teach our children to talk, but we cannot talk for them. Teach a person to fish, but do not give free fish too often, for it will surely remove his will and ability to provide for his family.

Each of you is a messenger of love and service. Be careful in the way you share your gifts with others. Giving to those who are unprepared can slow down their spiritual progress, as well as your own.

The Law of Freedom

Freedom is in the realm of the non-power. There is a multitude of ways to feel freedom and only one way to attain it. The Way of Truth has changed the term "Soul Journey" to "Universal Soul Movement." To gain the first phase of God-Realization and experience the bliss that accompanies it is only one preliminary step to understanding the freedom that goes with it. The full embodiment of freedom occurs when the God seeker understands that his or her mission must coincide with the Best-Laid Plans of Sugmad's Universal Soul Contract. It (Sugmad) comes into this void with a mission as well. Some God seekers gain God-Realization and become dysfunctional. They overlook the necessity of understanding there must be a shift from universal singularity to quantum universality. This is the reason why we have changed our transition of consciousness to "Universal Soul Movement." This term entails the full scope of God-Realization. Once an individual attains God-Realization, they must begin to inquire with Sugmad on the nature of their mission. Their attainment is not permission to start a new theology or path. All paths and theologies are guided by the plans of the Silent Nine and to start a venture without having it written in Sugmad's Contract will mean the person will take on the karma of those they are misleading. Attaining God-Realization is only one leg of soul's voyage. When the mind surrenders, it can know the freedom of Soul.

All of life's lessons ultimately lead us to freedom in the Heart of Sugmad. The Law of Freedom upholds the Creator's ability to transcend creation, to know Self in its entirety by knowing fully any and all of Its parts. You must give freedom to others to have it for yourself. Freewill is Sugmad's gift to ALL life, and in the human body, soul must adhere to the directives of DNA, and is bound by it; DNA and your birthplace set the stage for your personal and collective karma, the protocols of your culture, the call of your soul and your Contract made with Sugmad to live a certain way in this lifetime.

It is soul that is free. The true question becomes "How well do you use your Free Will to uplift your life and the lives of those you love?" Hence, you create your destiny and the destiny and balance of planet Earth.

The Law of Noninterference

This law states no soul may interfere in the Free Will and choice of another; to do so destroys that soul's ability and right to choose and grow into the true love and service to Sugmad. Each soul is given its own attributes, original cause and trajectory into life, and abilities and challenges to endure, solve and overcome.

This law brings up an important concern for all of humanity. World governments have been dumping contaminated refuse in our waters and burying it into our earth without recycling. Nuclear tests under and above our Earth's crust are disturbing the plates our civilizations are resting on. The debris from this waste matter is now residing in our atmosphere creating "global-warming" cumulatively over time. It is more serious than we have been led to believe. I will need the collective consciousness of the Light and Sound's participants to help me avert a catastrophe. Right now, floods and droughts are in the process of unleashing themselves because of humanity's interference with nature's God-given processes. It will be in the daily practice of our contemplative exercises. Spirit will use each of us as a conduit to avert world disaster. Humanity as a collective consciousness has been in direct violation of this law. It is the mission of The Way of Truth to bring this planet back into balance through the adjustment of this planet's vortices with the help Sri Tindor, Sri Leytor, Kusulu, Arutu, and many other teachers of our beloved path, and it is collectively one of the purposes of our Universal Retreat as well as bringing Africa to its next stage of Spiritual Renaissance. Species of life are being affected by "global warming" and it has been proven scientifically how one species is integral to the interconnection and unity of ALL life. Do everything in thought, action, coin and feeling with the intent to serve Sugmad. In this way, you incur no karma, and help heal our planet.

The Law of Unity

Soul exists in the wholeness of Sugmad. This unity entails all creation, great and small in all its uniqueness and diversity. Open your heart and you can feel this "Universal Oneness." Salvation is now, and moving with the flow of ALL life connects you with the glory of the God Worlds.

Contemplative Prayer

Contemplation is the mind and soul's ability to focus on and connect the participant with the Word of God. The process of contemplation is ongoing. Sit still singing Inwardly or Outwardly a mantra or holy word and/or repeat holy words Inwardly throughout your day. Contemplate the moment and seize the day. Do not allow the Outer world to distract you and your connection with Spirit.

Contemplative Exercise

I will be taking you on a movement of consciousness through a contemplative prayer.

1. Close your eyes and gently focus on the matter by inhaling and exhaling air. Know and understand even the air has intelligence on the sub-atomic cellular level. Know and understand you are inhaling millions of years of collective knowledge into your consciousness.

2. On the out breath sing aloud or silently; "*AH-LA-HU*" and then visualize yourself taking in oxygen and breath-sustaining life and this plant's collective knowledge with the in breath.

3. Now ask Sugmad to give you more compassion and love for this planet and ALL life on it. Pause for a minute.

4. Now ask - if It chooses to answer you, ask a question of any type of spiritual inquiry you choose - a direction in life, a solution to a problem, or a creative project.

5. (Silent contemplation for two minutes.)

6. Open your eyes and let's not close the flow; allow it to reside in you for the time being to understand how to identify this frequency of spiritual flow.

Sunday session

The Fundamentals of the Contemplative Life

The Light and Sound- Foundation of ALL Life

Sugmad is the first cause of this universe, and It is the Light and Sound that is It's primary emanation. Waves of varying frequencies and wavelengths descend from Sugmad, illuminating and amplifying energy motion. Light and Sound is the life-force and source of all life and religions.

Each plane of existence descending from Sugmad Itself generates a different frequency and calibration of the Light and Sound. Your continual use of the spiritual exercises will prepare you for mastery of the God Worlds. Master the exercises and you will master your soul's Life Contract and destiny. This is all a part of Sugmad's Love and Grace. Mastery of the exercises will open the Gates of Heaven. Open the heart, free the mind, and allow "Universal Soul Movement."

Soul was placed in a physical body to develop in a multi-dimensional universe in order to confirm without doubt, its own existence. We were sent here to enjoy and know the physical world to experience our full range of love and wisdom and to witness and live the extremes of life: fullness versus deprivation, abundance versus poverty, intelligence versus ignorance.

Sugmad created different planes of existence because It needed to experience, as we have need to experience; Sugmad needed to reflect upon Itself so It created the God worlds for souls to understand and experience what it is like to be in God's essence, It's consciousness. Sugmad created the physical worlds so it could partner Itself with us in our daily life, in our play, in our joys, happiness, triumphs and sorrows. Sugmad wanted to be in us and with us in what we learn, love, and cherish. This is why the teachers who have walked this path like Jesus, Mohammed, Shamus Tabriz and Rumi have said, "See God moment to moment for It is with us."

Why God is Called Sugmad in The Way of Truth

Words and sounds carry energetic frequencies that imprint upon mind's and soul's collective knowledge. The word "God" has been used and abused by those who seek power over the minds and hearts of others. "Sugmad" has not been perverted and profaned thus far.

Sugmad and the Spiritual Hierarchies

Sugmad created a unique hierarchy of spiritual administration for each plane of consciousness for focus and specialization in order to carry out many unique duties that became required on each plane of consciousness. Soul is given opportunities to serve on each level of consciousness through initiations, a greater connection with Spirit and Sugmad, and direct assignments from the Living Sehaji Master.

Why Sugmad Created a Division between the Physical Worlds and God Worlds

In the God Worlds knowledge is universal; it is transmitted fully and received instantly. Love is ever-present. Souls in the God Worlds are joyful, jubilant and free, but souls cannot experience the full range of awareness and gain the full spectrum of the Light and Sound experience within the God Worlds of wholeness. So, the physical worlds were created to provide souls with a greater arena to learn and know more, as a learning laboratory for soul.

You must remember the lesson of "As above, so below." As each of you begins to develop a higher, spiritual understanding of yourself in "Universal Soul Movement" you will observe how your open heart will see the refined realms of the God Worlds, and will see Heaven is here and now; your destiny is here and now; and your spiritual liberation is here and now.

I would like to introduce you to a contemplative exercise in your spiritual materials that are forthcoming; it will be an exercise to guide you to the fullness of Self-Realization:

1. Close your eyes gently, we will sing "*HU*" five times; and then you will repeat with me a postulate to release the flow of Spirit:

    a. *"I see through the Eyes of Soul."*

    b. *"I understand that which I see is through the wisdom of the Masters."*

    c. *" I act upon this joy and love from the Heart of Sugmad."*

    d. *"I exist in perfect balance with the highest laws of God."*

2. Now listen to the choir of the HU.

3. (After quietude.) Now let us sing "*HU*" together five times.

4. Pause. Slowly open your eyes.

Towart Managi and the female Sehaji Master Arutu's Statement to Sugmad's Children of the Light and Sound:

"You are an important part of Africa's Renaissance. Let go of the waste of the past. To be here and now in Africa's Renewal means to grow in the fullness and wholeness as a seeker of God's Love. It means knowing who you are, what you came here to do, what you are willing to do, and by all means, knowing truly what you are capable of doing. It means lending a helping hand to your fellow human beings, no matter the color of their skin, the style of their clothes, sound of their music, lifestyle, culture or mindset.

If you believe, like [we] believe, that Africa is the heart, soul and mother of humanity; then how are you willing to help your mother? To be an integral part of this blessed awakening, you must be ready, willing and committed to waking up to who you truly are. You must be willing to accept your brothers and sisters as unique and different from yourself, equal and deserving of all good things, like you are.

If Jesus and twelve disciples can bring greater love in this world, is he not saying, that each of you can make a difference? Should any man or woman be denied a place at our Father's Table?

To heal the heart of this planet, we must heal our own hearts first. Start here, for this is where true healing begins. Forgive yourself, forgive others and you will begin the road to your freedom and eventually, open those doors for others."

Spiritual Exercise from Towart Managi

1. You may repeat this Inwardly or Outwardly. *"I devote my breath, heartbeat, and life's song to the Great One God. I open and live in this One Love, Here and Now. Let all my fears and concerns vanish like shadows in the Fullness of Light and Love. The Holy Spirit guides and protects me."*

2. Close your eyes.

3. Relax completely.

4. Imagine yourself standing with your Inner Master in a high point above the Earth, over our blessed Africa.

5. Looking down upon Mother Africa, see, feel and hear the Light and Sound filling your hearts, filling them with the rhythm of this planet's heart.

6. See the Light and Sound in various luminous colors surrounding the entire Earth, enfolding the Earth in radiant yet gentle tones pulsing with life and Love and encouragement.

7. Sing softly **"AH-SWAY-LO"** three times.

8. Feel Oneness in connection with the healing flow of Sugmad's Great Love into the Earth plane. Know that you are a true warrior of the Heart and conduit for Sugmad's love.

9. Open your eyes slowly.

10. End with, "Blessed Be."

Continue to feel and participate in the energetic exchange between the triad of three, the trinity number of Sugmad, also known as God, Earth and you, the God seeker. We are the three within three. All that is not love cannot stand the heat and energetic pulse of love; will wither and die; and be dissolved into the great stream of God's love pouring through you.

Know that the entire spiritual hierarchy loves you and wants you to succeed. Keep your Heart Pure, and in alignment with the Love and enrichment of all life.

The African Master of Olde, Kusulu

Kusulu is another master assisting and forging new areas of development for Africa's Renaissance. To many in this room, he has assisted you in the dream state, giving you solutions to the daily problems of life and new alternatives to a better life. I am going to share with you more about Kusulu's life after I share with you a story of a young participant of The Way of Truth who was looking for a husband to share the rest of her life with.

This young woman came to me telling me she was tired of being alone. She kept running into men in her life who were unkind in their words and actions and did not treat her as an equal.

I informed her that Spirit knows the ways of the Heart, but she had to let Spirit know what she wanted in a partner. I advised her to write in a journal what she needed emotionally from a partner. She did so, but I also asked her to write about what she could offer to the relationship with the right person. I wanted to emphasize it is important to know what we can offer that the person does not already have. A relationship is a balance of different talents and skills. For example, some men actually prefer doing the meals and allowing the wife to clean up after the meals. Traditionally, I mentioned to our female participant to clean up all the emotional and economic responsibilities she had before so he could enter her life. Consequently, she stopped going out with her girlfriends wasting monies on frivolous pursuits, paid off as many bills as she could, and began to keep her apartment neat and clean. She realized she did not want to bring in any burden unnecessary to a relationship. When she settled into the routine of cleaning up her own life a man walked into her life, swept her off, and soon thereafter married her. They have been married ever since. Love means we must always consider how karmic responsibilities affect the other person in our life.

Kusulu found it was important to develop his own creativity and not be concerned with what others thought of him. He realized he was not living for himself. He began to develop skills of insight to look and discern beyond appearances. He found it wise to express his feelings openly with kindness, yet with firmness. He used the contemplative exercises to accept and live in harmony with others different than himself, and to live with emotional agility, understanding, and compassion. Kusulu learned wisdom from the trials and errors of his life.

As he grew in the skill of "Universal Soul Movement" (the movement of consciousness out of body) without limitation, he gained universal access to all planes above the physical worlds, as well as the physical worlds themselves.

Kusulu wanted to mention that the great mystic Babaji often spoke with his students about the ego wanting to be a part of the "Universal Soul Movement" into the God Worlds. The mental consciousness is not capable of processing soul-knowledge above the Etheric Plane because the mind has a gravitational pull toward problems. If the mind has an imprint (a memory) it has the habit of repeating it until the person says, "I've had enough of this mental habit." There are few mental habits beyond repair. Like a mechanic fixing a car, the contemplative exercises give you the tools to repair whatever is going on in the physical consciousness.

The mind is like the engine and the electronics in the car, but it is soul who has the key and the heart is the ignition. The mind truly wants to understand the joy of living in God Consciousness, but it needs soul to give it guidance.

This is an exercise to allow the joy of living into your consciousness and bypass the mind. Babaji used this technique when a certain sadness fell upon his heart when he looked at how people treated each other without love.

A Contemplative Exercise that will allow the joy of living into Your Consciousness

1. Let us sing *"HU"* five times and we will go into a quietude – a stillness in the body - and we will focus on some memory that gave you happiness and joy. Keep putting a picture together, but I would like you to put background into the picture; so if it was a birthday party or family celebration; see the chairs, visitors, and food.

2. Feel how the food tasted; the idea is to put as much as you can in the picture.

3. Now that the picture is processing itself: repeat after me inwardly or outwardly *"NU-LETEN-NE."*

4. End the exercise with, "Blessed Be."

~ Sri Michael

The Way of Truth Universal Retreat

Baltimore Maryland

October 20-22, 2006

The path of The Way of Truth is a less-traveled road of self-discovery. It is a walk through existence for the courageous and spiritual warriors who want to walk the upper regions of God in their lifetimes. My talks afford me the opportunity to speak of areas of spiritual priority that cannot be simply grasped by words alone.

The Universal Laws of Sugmad

The Universal Laws organize the universal creative processes. Sugmad (also known as God) entered the void of this existence, and the Laws foundational to our universe were created with the intent of developing and educating soul. The Universal Laws insure balance and love's expanding abundance here with us "moment by moment."

The Law of HU, this universe's life code, pertains to God's heart and breath. To stand on the top of the mountain in God's Consciousness, you must abide fully in the total absorption of God's love for ALL life. The HU is the key to all universal love and wisdom. It is the stabilizing resonance of God's Consciousness that holds this universe in the present Sugmadic quadrant we are in. The HU makes substance of what is known in science as "anti-matter" and is the spatial gel that prevents planets and galaxies from colliding into one another.

The Way of Truth Eternal – Book I (Book I) in book form is available and the door to this spiritual commentary is somewhat detailed within its context. Our Holy Book II (*The Way of Truth Eternal – Book II*) is slated for release in December, 2007 and will completely give a full explanation of the understanding of the nature of existence and Sugmadic Consciousness.

The Law of Soul visibly unveils to the human consciousness that we are a part of God's fabric and essence. All things, beings with consciousness, have soul-substance. It gives credence to the giving of love, detached goodwill and compassion to all life without regard to the soul's personality or Life Contract.

The Law of Love is the key to opening the heavens. Its frequency in the heart consciousness is what opens each gate of Heaven in the God Worlds. Love aligns the soul's Contract with Life to its highest potential. Love makes adjustments to the waves of Light and Sound emanating from the physical body. Love sustains, regenerates and expands the bliss and peace found in human consciousness.

The Law of Karma in accordance with *Book I* is the greatest balancing principle that guides the life and soul, as it progresses along the path and learns the proper way to develop wisdom, knowledge and the giving of love. It is the wise blending of will, desire and action with the Holy Spirit that leaves no residual effect of negativity. This law leads soul to a higher understanding of its divinity. Soul can create from the Higher Realms of its own beingness and bring vibratory frequencies of Light and Sound into physical manifestation through the proper use of thought. The mind, overdeveloped in the mental processes and mathematics, without appropriate attention on soul, runs into rigid thinking and the inadvertent collection of negative engrams. These engrams are like "mind-pictures" spinning negative energetic effects on the seeker's life. Our verbal inventory of negative thoughts and words used in our world is a direct window to how they work to shift our consciousness from the bliss of living to undesirable states of consciousness.

For example, I knew of one God seeker whose moods and attitudes were directly affected by the verbal-words of others as well as her own. When certain words like shame, disappointment and the name of her boyfriend was used, she would go directly into depression. I was eventually approached about her depression and suggested she go into contemplation, using her personal word or HU, to uproot the negative pictures and energy behind those words. She ended up writing up a list of words she no longer wanted to use. After a reasonable period of taking these words into contemplation, and facing the repressed emotions attached to their verbal inventory, her mood swings and depression were brought under control. The words you use on a daily scale are a direct measurement of your personality and soul's evolvement. Picture and image love in every action you take and your words will reflect this choice of action.

Karma is also known as "cause and effect." You reap what you sow; what you give is what you get. This concept exceeds more than one lifetime. Our energy patterns have the trajectory force to move from one lifetime to the next. What we put into action today must exact itself with the balance in the universe. Most of the karmic patterns resolving themselves that many of you are experiencing arise from Ancient Egypt, Ancient Rome & Greece, to the 1940's in Germany and France. But the latter does not exclude the immediate manifestation of actions incurred from a prior action a day ago. Soul's Contract with life regulates the flow and constriction of Spirit and physical manifestation. Soul is a historical document that has the endless capacity to store and provide the human consciousness with information on its past lives. The mind is incapable of putting the puzzle of these projective forces together. When the soul extends its freedom, the mind retreats into its well-deserved servitude.

Soul integrates energy. The mind, if used properly, will distribute soul's wisdom without dissecting or analyzing it. Repetition of thought activity, much like rigid patterns of thinking, action and perception, can only be released by unconditional love, and this is willingness to give the heart its opportunity to express itself.

The Law of Soul acknowledges when soul is active; it will begin to scan material to include objects and human intelligences without attachment to what is seen or possible outcomes. This is the entry to using the "space-time continuum" for "Universal Soul Movement." Once fear is placed into a "sleep state," soul can accelerate the mind's "inner timing" and connection with the Universal Mind Consciousness and project soul movement along the time-line, folding time and space. Some of our participants are presently retrieving past life information for the purpose of resolving their lack of success in life, as well as their present illnesses. Discourse V will speak more of what I have just mentioned.

The true journey of life begins with the empowerment of soul-awareness. God created to discover Itself through soul, thereby placing soul through many levels of development. In the reincarnative cycle, soul is given the seed of forgetfulness to insure its education is substantial. And soul is placed in denser and courser states of materiality and illusion to recognize its potential and eternal nature. Soul is actually the same in nature and structure as God, for it is an intuitive-reductive unit of God. Soul begins its journey to become more individualized and specialized in nature to experience its singularity, its heritage as one of God's children, and universality as a totally absorbed conduit of God's love. The soul who has reached this level of God-Absorption must be vigilant in maintaining humility, compassion and service to the Best-Laid Plans of the Grand Council, a revered group of souls managing the balance of this universe in their selfless duty to God.

This reincarnative cycle allows soul to express all of its creativity. No soul can do all it seeks to fulfill in one lifetime.

Soul is given "Free Will" to choose how it wants to direct itself and its physical encasement. Soul comes into a contractual agreement that specifies its mission and its family, social and creative dynamics. When soul understands its Life Contract, it can move, negotiate and change critical areas of its life. Know thyself and the world becomes crystal clear. Soul's movement into further clarity of itself is a direct alignment of energy with God's expanding knowingness.

One of the most expedient means of understanding your life mission and agreement with life is daily contemplation. It is an active form of engaging the mind in activity aligned with soul. Contemplation is closing the eyes and placing focused attention on the Middle Eye, also known as the Pineal Gland. And the God seeker will sing HU, an ancient name for God, or any word of reverence they carry within them. It could be the name of "Jesus" or any spiritual name close to their heart. Practice of the daily contemplative exercises will relax the mind and its hold on soul's communications to the participant. The rest is a matter of listening to one's heart.

I would like to invite each of you in a contemplative exercise that has been used to learn more of your life-mission, Soul Contract and Outer creativity.

Life Contract Contemplative Exercise

This exercise comes from the book *The Discovery of Self*, slated for release in March, 2007.

1. For those who would like to try this exercise, close your eyes. Focus your attention on the "Middle Eye," the spiritual doorway between the eyebrows.

2. Release the mind; inwardly see relaxation going through your body deeper, deeper, deeper.

3. Then call upon the Inner Master, or any beloved spiritual guide of your choosing.

4. Imagine a blue veil being lifted off your heart and removed from your Third Eye, awakening all your Inner senses and opening your attention-awareness to a greater understanding of your life.

5. Ask to know your Life Contract; you will repeat after me this mantra; it means "**All of which is God, is also in me.**" Let us now begin: "***A-LA-TU-SEN-TA***." Each phonetic part of this mantra will be sung and the entire mantra three times.

6. Listen to the sound of love and joy from the Inner Planes; look for the wisdom within,

Focus on surrender to and feel a radiant love pulsing within the center of your beingness.

7. End the exercise with, "Blessed Be."

The more you practice this contemplative exercise, the easier it will be for soul to communicate with you.

Spiritual Laws Supersede Humanity's Laws

It took "men of God" to protest the injustice of laws in the United States that prohibited people of color to attend schools of their choice and laws that dictated where a person could eat, sleep or live. If we were left with just society's laws, our world would be in chaos. Unlike manmade laws, the spiritual laws are written into the fabric of our hearts.

Spiritual laws are immutable, eternal, and serve the interests of all concerned. Humanity's laws serve the Outer world and are subject to the capricious whims and directions of human lawmakers. Human laws may be born of love and desire for protection, but it will take men and women who are guided by their hearts and a commitment of true service toward humanity for these laws to achieve fairness. Humanity's laws will always be a "work in progress" and in continual refinement to balance the soul-group's collective consciousness.

The Law of Love

Love is what sustains us, sustains our universe; and is the prime directive and life essence of God. Love permeates and transmits life-codes, moves and uplifts, gives joy and pleasure; wholeness and connection. The Law of Love shows us that in order to be in alignment with God, we must imbue love in every waking moment and in action.

The Law of Compassion

We must invest love into all circumstances. We can stay in harmony within ourselves even though we have a certain dislike for certain events and actions. Giving goodwill without conditions keeps us in compassion. It is through the use of compassion that soul can remain in integrity while giving freedom to others without involving ourselves in their emotional upheavals. Love is the essence of all life. Compassion opens the doorway to the giving of love "moment by moment."

Forgiveness and God's Everlasting Grace

It is natural for souls to differ in their needs and modes of expression. Forgiveness is a recognition of soul's need for experience, even if it leads to error and oversight in action and judgment. Forgiveness cleanses the human vehicle and strips away the dross of the soul and of the heart. Forgiveness is one of soul's greatest acts of charity. You see; charity is a gift of love without strings attached. To give is to receive. Forgiveness cleanses the ego and human mind of attachment and vanity. Look for the positive, no matter how dark or painful the situation might be. The negative polarity cannot endure or even exist without the positive side of life holding it up. We are in large part, our neighbor's keeper, because what we do outside our home does affect other people. A smile uplifts and sends a charitable gift of love, and it ripples an energy love into the Inner and Outer worlds of love.

These infinite laws all speak of "Love of God for God," "Love of God for creation," the Love of God for individual souls; the Love of self for God, the Love of self for creation, and the Love of self in recognition of God being in each of us.

The Law of Silence

Silence is embedded with love and strength. Silence holds great energetic frequencies of Light and Sound. It is human nature to share, to give and to receive, to move the tremendous energies inherent in our own beingness. We must learn to release emotional and mental energies with responsibility, without reaping "cause & effect" in their expression. One must master the art of becoming adept at holding and channeling these internal, powerful, and often unimaginable amounts of energies.

Silence has a direct relationship to the Law of Economy, because silence conserves the energy of the righteous. In silence you are able to make maximum use of your energy without waste. Every thought and action becomes foundational to and builds upon the next series of life experiences. Every act of love leaves a critical impact and changes life in an integral way. Every smile becomes a beacon of light and every day carries a new beginning. Economy of action breaks karmic loops – repetitive cycles of unwanted events, people and emotion.

The mentoring of the Archangel Gabriel in the use of silence opened the Gates of Heaven for Rama, Mohammed, Saint John of the Cross and many other wonderful teachers of this Earth.

Quetzalcoatl, Master of Olden Times

Quetzalcoatl, one of our teachers of the Light and Sound, will be awaiting a majority of the participants here to work with you in Ekere Tere, The City of Light. His teachings will consist of tutoring you in Divine Love and developing its attributes: devotion, compassion and trust in spirit.

Women were very instrumental in his preparation for mastership. They helped him in the virtue of surrender to Sugmad's Will. Quetzalcoatl's spiritual experiences began at age four and were greatly encouraged by his adoptive mother and his birth-mother who died giving him life. Archangel Gabriel was a guardian, a major mentor and protector of his dream state, who focused his study on readjusting world consciousness more on unconditional love and working with the Sehaji Hierarchy of the White Robe.

Quetzalcoatl's Contemplative Exercise for the Removal of Illusion from Your Living and Spiritual Environment

1. Let us sing *"HU"* five times and then allow Spirit to fill your heart with love.

2. See the blue wave of the HU enter your body and move into your heart.

3. Now say inwardly as I say outwardly *"Sugmad, I am coming!"* Say this three times.

4. Now see yourself with any spiritual master of your choosing standing next to a river in the God Worlds, called "The River of God." This river consists of molecules of white and gold Light and Sound.

5. Allow the spray of the river's flow to wash away your fears, your doubts, anger and attachments; and any obstacles between you and Sugmad.

6. Let yourself be cleansed Inwardly and Outwardly.

7. Now repeat *"Sugmad, I am coming!"* inwardly with great joy and anticipation.

8. You may open your eyes and feel Sugmad's loving embrace. And welcome home.

Sunday Session

Universal Soul Movement

Welcome! Our brothers and sisters of the Light and Sound bid you love and salutations from their gathering in the ancient Valley of Tirmir. Milarepa gives recognition and appreciation for the sacrifices you have made, coming to this momentous retreat.

The Way of Truth's commitment to teaching you the various degrees of Universal Soul Movement is an ongoing process that expands with the expansion of Sugmad's Consciousness. Universal Soul Movement is a projection of the Soul Consciousness, which allows it to move backward and forward on the Time Track. The future of soul is a set of probabilities; being here and now confirms what is real and what exists. Some experiences must occur, but there are some we can simply shift out of our space. How you choose life-experiences can either accelerate or slow down the pace of soul's movement on the Inner and the Outer.

When you have gotten to a place where life is even, nothing exciting is going on and there appears to be no major impediments or obstacles occurring, Soul is informing you that much karma behind you in time has been resolved. Soul is requesting you to make some new creative choices to initiate further movement. Universal Soul Movement is also a balanced cooperation of the Soul and Mental Bodies moving forward in time to prepare states of consciousness and events to choose from. This is also a beautiful aspect of completing life-cycles. This is the reason many of us have actually initiated two to three different careers.

Universal Soul Movement moves the participant from the singular to the universal. This means every action is seen, perceived and felt as a movement with Sugmad (also known as God.) In using your holy words and mantra to go into contemplation, see what you want and see yourself partaking of the scenery that is being created. Hold those images for several weeks, and release them with the confirmation that they are true; they are real and they serve the interests of all concerned.

Universal Soul Movement is an active use of projecting thought and Soul Consciousness, with the intent of achieving Self-Realization and God-Realization. With Universal Soul Movement; there are levels of spiritual absorption you will experience. This absorption purifies the personality and personal perceptions and emotional and mental habits. In ways unobserved by us, our friends, family and loved ones will tell us they see something wonderful and uplifting in our hearts. Universal Soul Movement develops prophecy and the ability to see within the hearts of others, and enables us to give and say what is needed to mend a heart, a hurt, or a disappointment.

Remember to focus on what you are earnestly striving for in life. Do not expend time on what you are trying to avoid. Attention and focus polarize energy around whatever object you are creating in your consciousness. Anti-matter is another foundational force of universal creation. It is a polarity of force that prevents sub-atomic atoms from welding together. Universal Soul Movement and God Consciousness utilize reference points of anti-matter around the magnetic field of the God-Seeker that can repel the negativity out of the participant's physical and spiritual environment without effort.

The age-olde postulate of "Be here now" means taking the "seeing element" of soul to create. "See only the thing you want, gently exclude all other matters." Refer to pages 84-89 of *Book I* for further elaboration. The area of anti-matter and the principle of cohesion are embedded in the Law of 9D in Kadmon's chapter in *Ekere Tere, City of Light*. For those who venture on with further interests, use the Merkaba technique in this book's chapter and ask your questions; spiritual, scientific or otherwise.

The imagination is projective; it is a projection of energy that moves outwardly into the world and toward others. We are in a universe of souls who depend on one another for love, support and cooperation.

This is an exercise that develops a revelational clarity of what you want in life. This exercise heightens the reality of life.

This is a step by step contemplative exercise that will assist participants in finding their spiritual mission and purpose.

1. Visualize yourself standing on a beautiful mountaintop surveying all the countryside and your life from beginning to end.

2. Feel the embrace of Sri Dan Rin and another spiritual master of choice with you.

3. Bring in Sugmad's Presence by simply inviting It. Then SEE the three of you making a powerful trinity in which you may move in the direction of your heart.

4. SEE the heart opening like a flower to the rays of the sun.

5. Let us dance – we three together with you in the Middle Eye- with all hearts wide open, connected, and flowing with Sugmad's great love.

6. Let us sing *"BEL-LA-HU"* together in joy and recognition and celebration! Allow Spirit's flow to take you with it.

7. Allow your purpose to come into your Inner sight and fill your heart with gladness.

8. Allow quietude for 20-30 minutes or until Spirit sees otherwise.

9. End the exercise with, "Blessed Be."

10. Be sure to write down your experiences so the joy and realness of this experience will not slip away.

11. Do this exercise daily for two to three weeks and remember Spirit can be subtle and sometimes, not so subtle.

Welcome to your true spiritual mission and cause. Welcome to the kindred spirits of the Sehaji!

Blessings and Love HU,

~Sri Michael

Module Three:

2007 Sehaji Transcripts

"The Beauty of God's Reciprocity"

The Way of Truth Retreat

Atlanta, Georgia

March 24-25, 2007

Saturday, March 24, 2007

The Beauty of God's Reciprocity

Climbing the summit of God requires God seekers to use their mental faculties. These are not our highest faculties, but yet are necessary aspects of the material world. It is the heart pumping the blood throughout the physical body that is the key to all awareness and knowingness.

The mind is a "necessary good" to humanity and is extremely capable of directing the body to an extraordinary level of physical achievement. The mind consists of two aspects: the mental consciousness and the Mental Body. The mental consciousness is the collectivity of memories and events from past lives. The Mental Body is the shell that can be seen, felt and intuited; it is the cup that holds together the memories. The Mental Body has material, projective force if it is directed with focus and concentration. See **Diagram A** (on next page.)

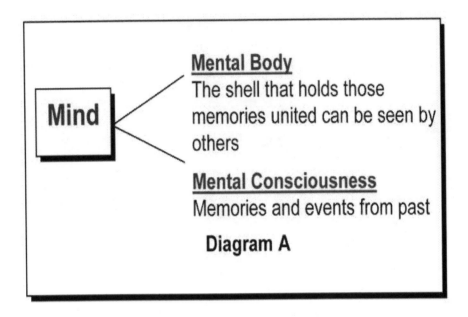

Mind

Mental Body
The shell that holds those memories united can be seen by others

Mental Consciousness
Memories and events from past

Diagram A

The challenge most God seekers encounter is recognizing the difference between the Mental Body and Soul Body. The mind can be brought to its highest capability if the Mental Body is used under proper, daily discipline. See **Diagram B.**

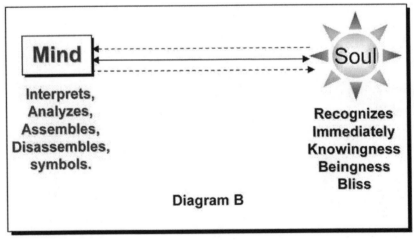

Mind

Soul

Interprets,
Analyzes,
Assembles,
Disassembles,
symbols.

Recognizes
Immediately
Knowingness
Beingness
Bliss

Diagram B

The Mind as a Perceptual Filter

The mind is brought to a calm after a long standing period of practice. The idea is to have the mind internally look like a clear pond. You want to be able to see what's at the bottom. In the same vein, you want to see what is at the foundation of your thinking. What ails the mind may exceed a lifetime. As soul, we bring in memories and the Mental Body is an excellent tool to retrieve past-life memories. The mind is the last stop for the memory to ground itself into the Physical World.

The mind holds up our problems and challenges. The daily contemplative exercises eventually bring about discipline of the mind. Emotions such as grief, sorrow, pain and memories that reinforce lack of self-esteem begin to naturally fade of their own accord. The mind has the tendency to analyze and break down what it is given. The mind must be trained, and stilled like a clear pond. Once this mind-picture is attained, it is ready to project forward and/or backward in time. The "still pond" is a movement of consciousness and an activity of thought. Without the discipline, the mind creates problems because of its need for creativity. It is for this reason that most savants and prophets considered problems as "illusionary." See **Diagram C** (on next page.)

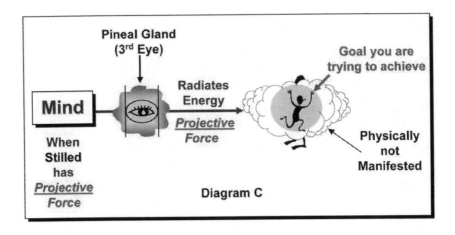

When the mind places a challenge before you, chant the sacred word "HU" and give the mind an errand to complete in the future. Giving love to yourself is the same as giving love to your mind; make it your friend. The mind wants to be useful. When we speak negatively of ourselves, we are giving the mind free license to do anything it will.

Master Rama of Olde

Master Rama's major obstacles were hesitancy, fear, and lack of confidence. He had difficulty resolving the subtle, subconscious labyrinth of ingrained fears gathered over lifetimes. The greatest cloak of fear he had to overcome was that of making mistakes. He found mistakes were not a mark of failure, but a method of mining experience for wisdom. Procrastination continually derailed his goals, but through the uses of spiritual exercises to integrate a line of cooperation between his mind, heart and soul, he finally found his way. Rama was always prone to distraction and had what would be termed today as "attention deficit disorder." Rama's Mental Body served him not as a friend, but as a distracter. The distractions served to get his attention, helped him focus and allowed him to make his mind his friend. Rama's failure to observe the Laws of Silence and Balance brought him a flurry of pain and suffering. He integrated his mistakes with the gems of wisdom found therein, and transformed all the muck and mire into a pure lotus of love, compassion and wisdom. Rama's determination and full integration of mind, heart and soul led him to Heaven's Gates, into the God Worlds, and into emotional and spiritual mastership. He wanted each of you to know that there is no limitation to God's Grace, forgiveness and love.

The Mental Body has the capacity to project itself into the past, present and future. Its highest maximal use is in the potential future movements of your Self. The use of the spiritual journal and writing down your goals automatically sends the Mental Body on a physical task. This practice is a good first step in training the mind. The mind needs to know your intentions and goals. Contemplation gives you an opportunity for "Inner dialogue" with it. Over time, it will become acclimated to a high facility of direction and productivity. The mind needs to know your priorities and gain a sense of when you want these tasks done. See **Diagram D.** (on next page.)

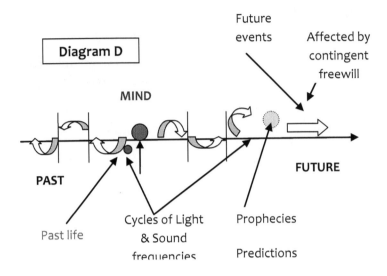

Diagram D

Future events
Affected by contingent freewill

MIND

PAST

FUTURE

Past life

Cycles of Light & Sound frequencies

Prophecies

Predictions

In contemplation, there are three reference points of energy being developed: the Physical Body in a reflexive activity, the Mental Body doing a physical task in the past, present or future, and in pure Soul Consciousness with heart and soul in direct cognitive processing, meaning there is an undisturbed connection between heart and soul.

Wherever the mind goes, the emotions will follow. The Mental Body leads; the Emotional Body follows. The Emotional Body will change to accommodate where the Mental Body resides. The constant projection of the Mental Body creates a "facsimile alignment" of agreement between the chakras and Inner Bodies of the human shell. The chakras will begin to open and close in higher frequencies of Light and Sound, and as a result of this action, unwanted habits and personality flaws begin to fade away effortlessly. Feelings of inadequacy and low self-esteem will simply disappear over time.

The Universal Mind Consciousness regulates time and time affects each person differently. In essence, one event can vary in duration from one person to another. It is our individual affection to the event in progress that slows down or speeds up time as we know it. For example, compare going on an errand you enjoy to one you generally have no affection for. Time will differ.

A Contemplative Exercise for the Mental Body

Let us do the exercise I have included in The Way of the Warrior, Discourse VI. I will abbreviate some parts of it for our Blessed Retreat.

1. When you close your eyes, I want you to bring a calm into your body.

2. Visualize this calm as a "clear pond."

3. Let us now sing *"HU"* five times.

4. Call forth the Inner Master or any Spiritual Teacher of your choosing. Now bring in the facial image of yourself, which you identify as your Mental Body.

5. Ask the Inner Master to give you guidance in the use of this exercise.

6. Visualize the picture of the goal you want to achieve. Place the picture into activity; this is not a "still shot." See the Inner Master working with you in this activity. If by some chance, the picture stays in a "still shot," the Mental Body is telling you to refine your picture; your awareness is overlooking some detail. Internally ask questions until the picture begins to move.

7. While in this contemplation, at this point we will use the mantra **"SA-YAR-TI"** for 20 minutes.

8. Upon concluding the exercise, tell the Mental Body that it will stay in the vibration of this contemplative exercise throughout your day.

Practice is key to the success of the Mental Body's use. All negative thoughts have a reference point in the past. Consistent use of the Mental Body dissipates emotional imprints of grief, disappointment and heartbreak. Consistent use of the Mental Body leads to development of the trance state for Soul Records reading. Some participants will be able to read the entirety of their reincarnative records and engage in spiritual prophecy. Monitor your journal to examine your changes in perception and awareness. You will also want to see how your goals are being fulfilled. *You must follow up this contemplative exercise with physically moving into what is needed to materialize your goal. For example: "looking for jobs."* Seeing within is a state of Beingness; every picture is a matrix of energy and a potential bridge into "present reality." The Mental Body can move backward and forward in time. When you visualize a picture/experience, ask the Mental Body to change the picture if there is some emotional weight tied to it. If forgiveness is required, direct the Mental Body to construct a picture of your asking someone's forgiveness. Our quality of life improves when our mind loosens its grip over our emotions. This exercise breaks "karmic loops" (reoccurring life situations.) For example, one female God seeker was looking for the right man... [A detailed story example was provided of this principle at work.]

Sometimes it is our thinking patterns that keep us from seeing "The Beauty of God's Reciprocity."

The Way of the Heart

The heart has a consciousness of its own, although its voice is softer. The heart's wisdom and knowledge is deeper and is indeed more far reaching than the undisciplined mind. If Earth's leaders were led by the "awakened purity" of their Hearts, this planet would be an oasis and a safe haven for humanity's far distant cousins. The higher use of the heart can achieve in circumstances where the mind wouldn't dare to venture. The heart is the nesting ground for love, the ground switch for higher consciousness, and the conduit for Divine Love.

Love is the essence, the energetic signature, and the creative expression of God. Love fuels and sustains all the worlds; it creates creation and manifests whatever it beholds. Love is Pure Spirit and Pure Spirit is love; Pure Spirit is Love in Its highest attribute. There would be no life in God's worlds without the all-encompassing power of love.

Love is the greatest power in purity and strength; it is the highest expression of living within "The Beauty of God's Reciprocity." It is the measure of your heart that guides the highest use of one's Free Will.

Love between man and woman is and was created to be a sacred expression of God's reciprocity as a spiritual expression of giving and caring between equal souls. The sacred bond created is built into the DNA of the animal kingdom and this DNA is transferable intelligence. Love perpetuates a reunion of opposites and is that which holds the "yin and yang" in unity.

Yaubl Sacabi, a spiritual master of olde, once said: "Ye shall see through the compassionate heart of the women God seekers that there is beauty in all things far and wide, and well beyond the limited mind of the Lower Worlds that struggles with ego."

God's channels assist in the development and maintenance of universal vortices of spiritual-physical power through their daily contemplative exercises.

What I have been leading to is the balanced integration of mind, heart and soul. Life's events and challenges often require the use of their combined consciousnesses. The higher use of this combination creates a "trinity consciousness," an expression of divine wisdom and love. A preliminary state of "Silent One" consciousness begins to develop once the participant combines this integration with the vigilant use of The Law of Silence. It is in silence where the voice of the heart can be heard with clarity and is where we come to know its intent. See **Diagram F.**

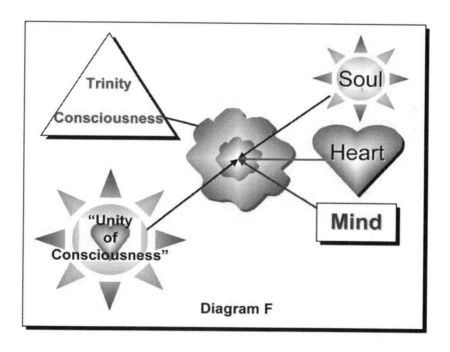

Diagram F

All races and beings bear kinship toward their own; the heart holds the connection to the God power and directs this love below the Great Divide to all living creatures both intelligibly and instinctually.

Creative manifestation works at its optimum with balance. Our messages to the hearts of others will reach their destination without interference. Our open hearts carry "The Eternal Laws of God" whether they are universal or specific to the participants receiving them. When the pure heart expresses Itself, truth emanates from It. Truth is the voice of existence and existence relies on truth to inform those who inhabit the Lower Worlds how things function and what must be done to keep all cycles moving and the universes alive, breathing, and expanding. We can see beyond the illusion with our hearts and see the truth in every moment of living. The truth is the energizing seed of liberation; it is the ray of Light that dispels the darkness, and is the gateway to everlasting life.

It will be the heart that will lead you to your mission in life. It is God's communication line to Its sons and daughters. The heart and The Eternal Truths remain unchanged throughout the universe and transcend space and time. Though the races and species differ in language, culture, and physiology, Truth remains the same, and it is the love that moves through our heart centers that has kept this world from self-destruction.

Arutu of Africa

Arutu, the famed female spiritual master of Africa, grew up in a family well established in the Ways of the Heart and into a royal lineage. The women of her day were often asked to walk behind their men and abide by their every word. Her own spiritual development led her to question the servitude that was her role as a woman to accept.

Arutu's spiritual lessons of life came directly from the peoples to whom she belonged. She inquired into the deeper recesses of herself, and used a spiritual technique very similar to the Mental Body exercise we used. Integrating her Mental Body with the heart and soul was an expeditious route in dissipating fear and personality flaws. It gave Arutu a method of "seeing" what she wanted to keep within herself and what she wanted to let go.

Arutu states that each of you should focus only on God's love coming through your hearts, and to seek to give love to all. Some of you will be (and already are) leaders in your community by virtue of your God-given talents. You are modeling the true service to God's Best-Laid Plans for this planet. You are doing this through your daily contemplative exercises and your random kindness and compassion. Love has an exponential effect upon the hearts of others and this world we live in.

Love heals, and everyone needs love. No matter what our roles in life, we can nourish others by the simple act of giving love from the heart, without expectations or strings attached. Simple acts of compassion and caring, kindness and joy, harmony and acceptance uplift humanity and render more balance to our planet and are part of Best-Laid Plans.

A contemplative technique for expanding the Heart and its consciousness with more love follows.

A Heart Expanding Technique

1. Let us all close our eyes and send a calm to our Bodies.

2. Visualize the picture of the Inner Master or any Master Teacher of your choosing.

3. Let's sing *"HU"* five times.

4. (Quietude)

5. Now say: *"Let my heart be clear and open to the Voice of Soul."* three times.

6. Now listen to what ushers through your Heart (for a few minutes.)

7. Now say, **"I now hear the Voice of Soul; lead the way each day."**

8. End the exercise with, **"Blessed Be."**

Prayer for Seekers of the Heart

The way is long and treacherous
The road well curved and worn
Yet never shall you find it
The greatness you have sworn
For it is so well hidden
And never shall be revealed
Unless you truly are given
The key to move the stone.
I long have journeyed and stumbled
Along the dusty road
But never was I given
The wine to slake my thirst
Until I did discern
The secret that was hidden
Beneath my very chin.

For the key to certain greatness
Is not in lines of prose
Or mental games
Or clever tricks
Or power over kingdoms.
It is secreted and hidden,

Beneath the garland rose

That blooms eternal beauty

And always does it grow

Within the heart of champions

And those who travel home

And open of their hearts

To the greatness and are shown

The secret key to finding

The sacred Rosetta stone

That shall guide them in their fortunes

And never leave them poor

Or bereft of the love of God

For the heart is what is given

To aid all seekers home

And it must be loved and opened

If truth is to be won.

For this is the only way,

That God may welcome you home,

And into Its heart above.

~Sri Gopal Das, *The Way of Truth Eternal - Book I. pg.114*

Sunday, March 25, 2007

The Giving and Receiving of Love

We must treat our friends, family and ourselves as if we are tending our own Spiritual Garden. The expansion of consciousness through the reading of The Way of Truth discourses, books, and initiation manuals has a direct loving impact on those we care for. The family dynamic tends to run in parallel with our unfoldment, and affects the growth of the family's spiritual life. As in a garden, if the soil is fertile, the Inner workings of the heart center are balanced; the nutrients necessary for healthy plants and flowers to grow are present, so the garden will become a beautiful expression of life and love. It matters not if all the members share the same path, ideology or theology. It is the scope of Love's diversity within the family that models the highest representation of the Law of Love and Freedom. The participant taking the initiative to bless their home in the name of God fosters a cleansing of old family engrams. The inward singing of HU develops a strong heart-to-heart connection when we are holding their hands; are in eye to eye contact or are holding them in gentle embrace. You can also hold the image of the tetrahedron in the Middle Eye and communicate with your significant others heart-to-heart; in the silence, the non-power will manifest answers for the family in the midst of life's challenges and opportunities for growth and love. The recognition that Spirit is working on your behalf will become as normal as breathing; just stay with daily use of the contemplative exercises and the random singing of HU throughout your day.

There are two ways to look at your life as soul. First, look at the cause and effect relationships in your daily life. See what is working for you and what isn't. In your contemplations start asking questions about why there are areas of disconnection with your loved ones, at your work and in the world. Listen to what comes to your heart and do not allow opinions or judgments to enter the "Inner dialogue" that develops. Just listen. Once you feel soul's communication has concluded, then say to soul, "Show me what you have imparted; give me a picture I can See." Stay in contemplation for a few minutes until the flow of Spirit releases you to open your eyes. A second form of soul-inquiry is the seeking of the Inner causes of events to occur or happen. The Outer world of activity cannot exist and endure without the Inner world of activity. The vision into the heart and life concerns lie within the Inner Realms.

The Sugmad Consciousness Exercise

1. Let's close our eyes and reside into the Tranquility of Heart.

2. Let's *"HU"* five times.

3. Now into the vision of your Third Eye bring an entire picture of yourself.

4. Now envision rays of orange filtering themselves around and through you.

5. Now envision rays of blue filtering themselves around and through you.

6. Request a teacher of merit to be standing next to you.

7. See that both you and the teacher are looking at a massive whirlpool of Light; it is God (also known as Sugmad).

8. Say to Sugmad, *"Absorb me, make our hearts as One and reveal your gifts to me."* three times.

9. Sing *"Sugmad"* five times and then slowly open your eyes.

10. End the exercise with, *"Blessed Be."*

Ekere Tere – City of Light

Many participants are receiving full training in the classes in this spiritual city above Abuja, Nigeria. It is here in this city that our participants are reading and learning about their Soul Contracts in this lifetime. These spiritual warriors found that understanding God's plan is in the being and doing in life, and in seeing God's expression of beauty and love in each moment. We are continually challenged to live in Soul

Consciousness by living in the present and letting go of concepts, emotional luggage, and belief-engrams of the past. An expeditious way to always move into greater consciousness is to live in the vigilant use of the Law of Silence. This makes it easier to receive, and has an uplifting effect on others when we give.

While we are in the concept of "giving and receiving," some participants have asked me about longevity and good health. Longevity and health come from a combination of right attitude, right action, your Soul Contract and what you have agreed to carry in this life. Your heart must guide you in what this means for you. Choices and actions made in former lifetimes have a direct effect on your individual life-force, and let us not discount the grace given to each of us when we selflessly surrender to the non-power of God's Will. Also, let us not discount thoughts and intentions; they are the energy that makes our atoms move. The part we play in life matters as much as how we play it. Choose to do what God asks of you and it matters not what gifts are received. God's abundance is within your Heart and your gift of Life.

What we put in our human shell is equally important, and it reflects the makeup of soul's vision and development. Nutrition, good common sense and understanding that each of us has different food group requirements, and consuming fresh local foods and juices devoid of harmful chemicals and full of living enzymes will contribute much to good health. Clear water blessed by heart and word, and varieties of herbs, plants and oils, adequate rest and varied physical exercise are also vital to keep the physical organs and emotional attitudes in balance. Emotional and mental stimulation, and the control and elimination of waste on all levels are essential to good health and contribute to the quality of soul's creativeness. Allowing the seasons of the year and of life to come and go without holding onto what is passing contributes greatly to happiness and health. Do not compare yourself to others, for God has already given you, His child, His love and blessings.

It is an important to visit daily with God in prayer, in contemplation, and to develop serenity when Outer circumstances are not to your liking. Employ the courage to do what you can and surrender everything to God. Look at every daily action as a brush stroke on an artist's canvas, or as if you are creating a tapestry of you living life. These are some of the building blocks of longevity, good health and a rich spiritual life. These are certainly not all, as the dynamics of each individual are multi-dimensional and multi-faceted. Walk with appreciation and gratitude for what God has given you. There is no end to His Love and Grace.

The Soul Contract

On pages 140-143 of *The Way of Truth Eternal - Book I* of our Holy Books, the Sehaji chart out a lengthy summary of the Soul Contract, this is your agreement with life and your life-mission. Soul receives the lessons it needs to understand its mission in life. Each of us must go through many doors before we gain a clear understanding of It. Some of you are already carrying out your missions by being parents, teachers, artists, musicians, ministers, Catholic monks, or other participants serving Best-Laid Plans.

A Soul coming to grips with its mission in life begins the great awakening of it to the Worlds of God and Beingness beyond the Etheric Plane. This is where we come to the full realization that Self-Realization is the first fulfilling step toward God-Realization. Words cannot come close to the majesty of God's reciprocity in the conference of awakening Itself in you.

What we do with this direct experience is:

1. We begin to ask for Spirit's lead in the development of spirituality in our children. We want to give them freedom and love; but blend these laws with guidance and our wisdom of life. We understand they may not connect with our blessed path as adults, but we have the knowingness we have done our best in developing the Light and Sound in their hearts. Our children must experience life directly, and as parents we must allow them their experience. Each of us will know individually when we must speak our hearts about what they do and how they live.

2. We begin to ask contemplatively how we can give more love in our home. Bless your home and state,

"Let no thing, thought, or deed enter my home unless it is in accordance with the Highest Laws of Sugmad," then *"HU"* five times before you start your day.

3. We begin to ask Spirit and our Inner Teacher to give us the creativity of giving more love in our work environment and more compassion to those in supervisory positions. We never know the conflict going on in their hearts when they are told to lay people off who have families, children and a home mortgage to pay. Their hearts are often quite heavy and they need love and a kind word, as well.

4. We begin to bless every area of our lives, and see others ultimately as Soul. Know within yourself there is a spiritual renaissance developing, and this represents an awakening of soul amongst those who have connected with the Light and Sound worldwide and universally in other places.

5. We begin to see how the Light and Sound is raising each awakened Soul to their highest degree of spiritual expression. You will give love to those who spiritually slumber in accordance to the degree of their own hearts.

6. We will speak words of wisdom and love to those whose hearts feel frustrated and lost, and will plant the seeds of Its (Sugmad's) Infinite love within their Hearts.

7. We will see the sparkle of God's Reciprocity in everyone we encounter, and our hearts will connect theirs to the fruits that our Father who art in Heaven has provided for all Its Children.

8. God-Realization and its daily maintenance include bathing moment by in the ecstasy of Sugmad's Love. Let there be no barriers between Soul and Sugmad, even in the midst of life's daily trials, torments and challenges; to know this is to know eternal bliss.

Sugmad (also known as God) reveals fresh insights about daily life every time you visit Its heart in contemplation. It reveals why things happen and how to change our thinking or actions to move into a greater awareness and how to accomplish Its Will in our lives.

A Sugmadic Consciousness Exercise

1. Let's close our eyes, get comfortable and begin to focus on the screen of our Third Eye.

2. Let's sing **"HU"** five times, and allow Spirit to enter your mind, heart and soul as a "blue light of Sugmad's Love."

3. You may request any Spiritual Teacher of your choosing to stand next to you. We are standing next to one of God's Rivers

pouring down from the God Worlds into the Physical World. The river is spraying forth white and gold molecules of Light and Sound all over your Physical Body. It is cleansing you of fears, angers, doubts, attachments and any other obstacles that remain between you and Sugmad.

4. Feel yourself being absorbed into the river; you are now moving upward into Sugmad's Realm. Trust that you know the way home. Let yourself be cleansed inside and out. Delight in your purification and joy.

5. Now either say to your self inwardly or outwardly, *"SUGMAD, I AM COMING!"* three times. Keep opening your heart until your Soul has indicated you are home inside Sugmad's Realm. See, Be and exist in It always. You are home.

6. End the exercise with, *"Blessed Be."*

How One Gains the Knowledge and Love of Sugmad's Heart

I often open myself to this discourse, each and every day contemplating upon what is it like to be Sugmad - omniscient, omnipotent and all-loving in the Allness of what Is. I consider my health and the home It has given me, and the old friends, family and those of you It has given me to love. I give thanks for the food upon my table and the adoration of my beloved wife who has encouraged and inspired me in my Blessed work in our sacred mystery school, The Way of Truth. When I place my attention upon these gifts of life, my heart feels Sugmad's love.

Sugmad is the embodiment of all truth and thereby all questions referring to It come with Its answers, if you will but hold your heart close. The answers to all the big matters of life are found in the simplest elements of your day. Quiet the mind and give it credit for being the faithful servant it is, and be still in the pure essence of the resonations of your heart. Be grateful for the consciousness you have been given and accept the infinitude of Sugmad's forgiveness.

Ask the questions of your heart, say "**OH SUGMAD, YOUR HEART IS MY HEART, YOUR LOVE IS MY LOVE**," and read this poem:

Poem for Struggling Seekers

When the heart is open
And the love is pouring in
Then the seeker knows that
He has attained the place
Of perfect wisdom, truth and understanding
That shall guide him in his way

And to the final goal.
Yet along the way and journey
Many are the tests to be faced
And it is to the seeker
To continue in his ways
And not abandon the heart of truth and wisdom.

For the challenge is the discipline
And control that must be sought
To master the illusions
And the winds they do create
To take the seeker far afield
Of the goal that he does seek
And the truth and loving comfort
Of the heart of Heaven's gates.
And so, the key is vigilance
Of the bodies and their state
And perfect control and balance
Of all that they do say and do
To keep you from your goal
For discipline and knowledge
Truly is the key
And if the seeker continues
And always casts about
The eye of discerning observance

He eventually shall see
And be able to follow
The center path before his feet
And succeed in his endeavors.

~Sri Kadmon, from *The Way of Truth Eternal- Book I,* page 194.

Blessed Be.

~Sri Michael

"Africa – A Mother's Call to Its Children"

The Way of Truth Universal Retreat

African Seminar

August, 2007

(Sri Michael's talk was presented via video. These are his notes, verbatim.)

Africa, my Africa, greetings and salutations from The Grand Council, The Silent Nine and Sugmad for the personal work each participant has put forth in their commitment, service and love toward their daily contemplative exercises and use of the spiritual mantras in The Way of Truth. This has initiated a large scale positive, collective effect upon Africa's upliftment and salvation. Africa is calling for Its children to place this planet back into balance. And a key to this universal work is our commitment to our daily contemplative exercises, our spiritual classes, community, friends and family. Sugmad and the Sehaji Masters are able to utilize each participant as a channel for the Light and Sound, and for this planet's highest good.

Our path is a living doorway to the God Worlds in which we are able to maintain one foot in Heaven and one foot on earth. The key to this delicate balance between the physical and spiritual world is the Law of Silence. We have many in number, who are growing in leaps and bounds and are in the full capacity of Universal Soul Movement. What keeps the expansion of consciousness unfettered by ego is Silence. Silence is an expression of the God power and all are drawn to it. Prolonged states of stillness within bring forth the God Wisdom, Love and material action for needed change in your life. It takes time to hold the "silence within" and listen to the concerns of others without rendering judgment and opinion. Silence develops the heart-to-heart communication and bypasses ego. Silence is unyielding protection and allows love to work at its highest degree of human activity. Be still and know you are a mirror of God's Love.

Africa is the birthplace of humankind and the cradle of our civilization. The level of the frequency of the Light and Sound in Africa is the highest rate of manifestation on this planet, and this is why there is nothing under the sun that cannot grow in Africa. Be one with Africa's consciousness and the Grand Council with the practice of the contemplative exercises and the diligent study of the newly released discourse focusing on the "mind, heart, and soul." Historically, the Light and Sound path has always placed a concerted effort in conveying a high understanding of the heart and soul, but the mind was left on the back burner. It was not given the attention and merit it deserved. Mind works for heart and soul and wants to be integrated into a higher facility of cooperation with these two consciousnesses. This world is dependent on the Universal Mind Consciousness and we cannot turn our back on its use of the Mind to maintain the physical worlds.

Babaji

In Chapter Ten of the Babaji book *The Beginning Has No End,* this ancient Indian sage and teacher states that the mind wants to work with us and in our best behalf, but it wants to know what our needs and goals are. Prior to our discipline of the mind, it has been working on the mental impressions of habit, fear and limited thought processing; the result is low-esteem and aspirations not yet fulfilled.

The mind used in contemplation has a greater effect if it is used in a task or event in the future. The future's outcome has a more flexible dynamic than a situation looking at us in the present. This is the reason why keeping a journal is important and keeping a focus on your goals keeps the Mental Body on task. Without discipline, the mind will gravitate to old problems and create a repetition of some olde events recurring over and over again, which I call a 'karmic loop." These spiritual challenges can be overcome by giving the mind "future tasks" that uplift your life. You have to change a program in your Life Contract. Some are easier to change; it is a matter of not letting go of your goals and dreams, and keep your visualizations of a better life in your Middle Eye. This allows Spirit to co-partner its work with you.

When you come upon a challenge in life, see no difficulty; affirm no difficulty. Visualize yourself in your Middle Eye and say "How can I put more heart and move love in this situation? I will step aside from my mind, and allow soul to do its work." The Mental Body will hear you, and will allow soul to use it for a higher cause and purpose. The forthcoming workshops about the integration of mind, heart and soul will focus heavily on this area of spiritual action. It is the gentle hand of God's Love pouring through your consciousness that changes and transforms Life.

When stones are thrown, give love and go your way. When harsh words are spoken, give words from your heart. When your brethren are down on one knee, see within yourself God's hand lifting them up, and when you can see an opportunity to give God's Love through a glance or smile, do so and know that in that moment, your action could change a life.

To face the daily challenges of life I leave you with this prayer song from the Sehaji Master Prisca:

(In Memory of Prisca, the female Sehaji Master)

Come into my Heart, my Lord
I pray to you each day
Show me how to live life
While walking in Your Way

Help me to be Willing
To do all that you may ask
Guide me to Your Heart within

From there I do each task
Protect me from the dangers
Lying in my Mind and out
Show me how to surrender
All my fears and doubts

Lead me to let go
Of things that are not mine
And live forever in your joy
I will be forever thine.

Read this prayer out loud and sing five "*HU's*" thereafter and begin your day, and keep your heart open to Love and the lead of Spirit.

Africa, my Africa, I am always with HU and you.

Blessed Be,

~ Sri Michael

"Ekere Tere, City of Light"

The Way of Truth Universal Retreat

Columbia, Maryland

October, 2007

Saturday Talk

Ekere Tere, Blessed City of Light

Good afternoon and thank you for coming to this Blessed Universal Retreat. The central focus of my talk with you will be on the spiritual City of Light above the Nigerian capital city of Abuja. Great preparations were made to build this spiritual city and though this planet has many cities of this nature, Ekere Tere remains unique and special-in-kind. Ekere Tere is represented by a book bearing the same title and it features the primary spiritual teachers who choose to give classes at this recently built city. The spiritual vibration of Ekere Tere is spearheading Africa's Renaissance, but much is also contingent on humanity's collective Free Will.

I intend to elaborate on the teachings available to the participant and God seeker who chooses the high road to Self-Realization and thereafter, God-Realization. The gift of Self-Realization brings forth the knowledge of self as soul, and many spiritual gifts from past lifetimes of learning and life-lessons. God-Realization comes with the quantum knowledge of self as an infinite unit of God. The pure knowledge of the God Worlds and its knowledge of existence and creativity come into fruition in increments to the God seekers. And they become a Light of God acting as a channel of Spirit uplifting this planet Earth.

Dedication Poem to Ekere Tere:

The Jewel in the Lotus

Herein rises Ekere Tere
floating in the sky like a Lotus
resting on still waters
It is not bound to the Earth
It has no memory of History here
but of the wisdom of each life lived
The center of this Holy City is a Jewel
that shines into the Eyes of God

It reflects the secret heart of one's most Beloved
which illuminates the many rooms and halls
that awaits the rustling of feet,
the opening of doors, the raising of windows

All hands receive answers and no voice is unheard
One word drops like a ruby from the mouth of God
on all who will listen
That word is Truth, dear ones, Sugmad's Truth
Blessed Ekere Tere.

The Law of Silence and Milati

Milati's chapter on the Law of Silence in Ekere Tere will be very helpful to those God seekers who want to develop their personal abilities. It is only in prolonged states of silence's stillness that the seeker can tap the pure unmanifested Love of Sugmad's knowledge and heart. Milati states that silence refines the individual focus of what areas of their life requires refinement. The God Power expands in silence, and its majestic vibration reveals Itself in the stillness of the daily, contemplative exercises. Silence opens the hearts of others as well as one's self. Adhering to the Law of Silence is a mark of high soul development and the doorway to understanding the secrets of this universe. Sugmad's heart is not to be squandered in casual conversation; Its magnitude and Grace is to be expressed in selfless commitment and service to the Best-Laid Plans of The Way of Truth.

Silence gives invisibility of movement, purpose, accomplishment and commitment. It is the mounting energy of silence that is the rock and mortar of soul's survival, stamina and fortitude. Silence gives the participant protection from the limitations of the mind. Silence embraces the

Infinitude of life's beauty and uplifting experiences. Silence is always partnered with the highly developed power of discrimination. Growth requires disciplined preparation. The disclosure of information to souls unable to digest what they are given not only creates karma, but has the capacity of destroying a soul's Life Contract, causing turmoil and unnecessary suffering. Indiscriminate talk is like spending money without thinking about having a savings account. The breaking of the Law of Silence gives the violator an extension of uncomfortable life lessons and endless series of indeterminate vulnerabilities.

Silence opens the doorway for more focus, attention and discipline. It gives us time to look at ourselves and change the course of our life's destiny. Once the self is confronted during prolonged states of silence and stillness, healing of the heart begins and its aberrant parts begin to meld into a balanced wholeness of unity.

I studied with Milati during the entirety of many lifetimes and for three years of vigilant training prior to becoming the Living Sehaji Master. Take the lessons of Life as a gift of soul development and into the Silence of the heart, and you will be brought into the daily miracles of living life. Silence magnifies Sugmad's (also known as God's) DNA in you. Embrace Silence and become a co-worker with God. And always choose Love above ALL things.

Contemplative Exercise

This is a contemplative exercise with mantra that will appeal to the Lords of Karma for a release of a physical illness and an understanding of the life-lessons.

1. Sit in a relaxed position and focus your attention at the space between your eyebrows.

2. Breathe deeply and slowly. You may say the word "*HU*" or any mantra that brings peace and slows the breath.

3. When you are completely relaxed, imagine that you stand before a white stone temple on a hilltop overlooking the sea. There is a bronze door with a black handle; turn the handle and step inside the temple.

4. You enter a spacious, circular room filled with sunlight and the scent of myrrh and sandalwood. There, at a large oval table, sit the Lords of Karma.

5. They greet you and offer you a chair at the table, so you may take your seat among them.

6. You may simply and earnestly say *"Revered Masters, give me health and well-being. Allow me to be rescued from the bonds of this illness."*

7. Then you may say this mantra: *"SO LE TU SA VA AHE."* (pronounced as "so-lay-too-sah-vah-ahay") three times.

8. Contemplate for the next 15-20 minutes, keeping your attention at the point between your eyebrows.

9. Know and accept that you have been heard by the Lords of Karma.

10. End with three **"HU's."** True healing is understanding Sugmad's Grace and Love.

Peace Be with You.

Gabriel, Archangel and Head of All Angelic Orders

Gabriel and the Angelic Orders have always worked with the Light and Sound under a multitude of names and cultural traditions. Gabriel counsels Saint Germaine on his supervision and guidance of this planet's healing organizations and orders. Gabriel has been the primary mentor for this planet's saviors, prophets and saints. He is one of few souls seen continuously in the spiritual courts of the lower and upper universes. Gabriel mediates the plans of the Lords of Karma and the overlords of the planes of existence below the Soul Plane.

Gabriel also mentors the saviors, prophets and saints after they leave their present life-assignments and thereafter assists in the structure of their future spiritual assignments on Earth and/or in other species' life-forms in this infinite universe. Gabriel is one of this universe's chief architects of world and planetary theologies and beliefs. He has to have direct communication with Tindor Saki and the Silent Ones. Vortices of power have to be constructed around collective consciousnesses that share common grounds of reality.

Tindor Saki and the Silent Ones are responsible for the spiritual design and energy-plates that keep our solar systems and galaxies from colliding into one another. The quadrants of this universe have a system of physics not yet within the maturity of humanity's reach, and this mathematical understanding will be a foundation for the folding of time and space. The field of mathematics and traditional scientific approaches will have some Earth-shaking intersections with spiritual laws and homeopathy in the next fifty years.

The Lords of Karma are pacing mankind's development and coordinating it with the pace of life-forms beyond the ken of our physical eyes.

Parmenides

This spiritual teacher coined the name of this path of the Light and Sound "The Way of Truth" as I graduated from Gabriel's tutelage and continued mentoring. Those who choose to enter his classroom will find his talks all-inspiring and highly instructive on the mastery of universal existence and God-Realization.

Parmenides focuses on the Law of Unity, the Law of Opposites, the Law of Reversed Effort, and the Law of Existence. These specific laws are integral to the attainment of Self-Realization and God-Realization. The Oneness experienced by the participant dissipates negative circumstances and events of life; there is no separation from Sugmad's Love. Consequently, fear of the unknown cannot maintain a grip on the participant's consciousness and the negative engrams lose cohesiveness due to love's unyielding presence.

Law of Unity

This law acknowledges that all souls are made of the same eternal substance. Each soul is ignited with individual consciousness, giving diversity and inherent, genetic qualities to varying group consciousness. The Light and Sound has a direct and positive effect on our genetics. Contemplation tunes the participants into an understanding of their physical bodies, but that is a reflection of God's Oneness, for we exist as soul in It. The old phrase "Just be and see through the eyes of God" lends itself to the understanding of using the Law of Unity in everyday life. See no separation between yourself and others and life-events. Just see everything you experience as an extension of soul and Sugmad's love for you. And never relent in your perception of this law. Conceive that there is NO thing existing without Sugmad's Love and what you identify with is the Love that gives it life. Love is the only reality, and through your individual Free Will you are confirming what created this universe.

St. Francis of Assisi was a fine example of someone who applied this law in everything he did. Francis prayed and contemplated on the idea that his every act would be done in God's Name. God was his ideal to follow and he creatively absorbed himself into the ideal of Unity and Oneness. See only love in all things and Be love in what you experience.

Ekere Tere

Ekere Tere is the portal to what will advance the human consciousness. The consciousness of mankind literally stands at the precipice between Light and eternal darkness. Ekere Tere and Its teachers insure mankind's movement toward the Light. The Kal forces must balance the pure love from Ekere Tere and Africa is experiencing the direct clash of the two polarities of the positive and negative.

Ekere Tere provides a meeting place for all the great masters of all the world religions to have a universal summit to discuss world issues and affairs. The City of Light is like a magnifying glass gathering forces of Light consciousness; it represents this Sugmad's heart. It was Sugmad who ultimately chose its location over Abuja, Africa to be the doorway for the fulfillment of Its plans to balance this universe.

It is an ideal location for hierarchies of angels to work from. These angels have existed since the beginning of time and their influence has hovered over humanity's consciousness through the centuries due to mankind's call for their help and assistance. They cannot control the thoughts of humanity, but they can influence the universal consciousness. It is humanity's belief in their existence and in their power to preserve love that opens the way for angels to influence world events.

Kadmon

For ages now science has dominated the medical field; this has been to the partial detriment of humanity. The field of science does not take into account the invisible life of humanity – its thoughts and emotions, its past lives and karmic conditions. It relies too heavily on artificial medication that addresses only the symptoms and superficial causes of illness. True natural medicine crosses the bridge between the physical and non-physical aspects of man; it works in harmony with the flow of energy within the meridians of the human body. Synthetic medicine interferes with the delicate balance of communication among those grids of energy.

Technology and Nature

The present balance of technology and nature weighs too much on the side of technology. This Earth was equipped with remedies for every ailment known to man: in herbs, flowers, plants, leaves, grass, bark, and the list goes on. The first inhabitants of the Earth learned to work in harmony with nature to formulate their own remedies. Later, science developed synthetic drugs to replace organic medicine. It has had its usefulness as in penicillin, which has saved countless lives from bacterial invasion, but now we are too dependent on drugs that become toxic and break down the body's natural defenses. The balance must tip back toward natural medicine to allow nature and not just technology to resume its place in the advancement of health and longevity of the human race.

The balance of the human body energetically works in alignment with the balance of the physical universe – the microcosm works with the macrocosm. Therefore, all things in existence must be brought into a state of unified balance, starting with the Physical Plane and working up into the higher planes of beingness.

Ekere Tere is a ground breaking spiritual city that represents a shift back toward all that is good, wholesome and natural. It will revitalize the use of crystal energy for everything from healing to transportation. Twenty-first Century man has only begun to scratch the surface of the secrets and powers of this universe. My work involved the re-introduction of the lost teachings of Atlantis, Lemuria and the forbidden and nameless cities of Yor. Ekere Tere provides the vehicle for these teachings to reach the higher consciousness of man. God seekers of the highest purity of heart and soul will have access to this secret knowledge

Our Distant Cousins

There is an invisible gateway that separates our galaxy from foreign galaxies that are not part of this solar system. Only through this gateway can other forms of life enter our atmosphere. Each entity who wishes to enter the Earth's domain is carefully interviewed and screened by a team of highly trained representatives of the Red Dragon Guard.

Each entity must prove that their desire to study humanity is for a highly benevolent purpose that will be used in the advancement of universal brotherhood and understanding among the species. Many of the life forms who come here are from dying races and wish to study how to use the Emotional Body to perpetuate their kind and save it from extinction. Some of these races have no Emotional Body whatsoever. They are highly intellectual; their Mental Bodies are over-developed to the point that they lost their ability to procreate. There is no personal love or art of creativity; it is all science and technology. They procreate by the use of artificial embryos they create in their own laboratories. These embryos are not capable of love, thus, there is no culture in their society. The essence of what is art, literature and creativity of any kind comes from love. These beings live in a Godless world; they crave to fulfill their emptiness. And so, they come here to study mankind in hopes of bringing back color and beauty to their sterile environments.

Many races have been turned away; otherwise this Earth would have been overrun by errant, foreign entities wishing to do harm and leave devastation in their wake. Their planet's contact with existence is closely monitored and there are beings that are an integral part of this planetary evolutionary process.

Sunday talk

The Vision of The Way of Truth

The Way of Truth will always be a mystery school. We represent a pure state of the Light and Sound. Our path is the foundation of truth, knowledge, love and existence. Academically, the Light and Sound is the foundation of mathematics. Truth is in the Heart, in the air we breathe; there is nowhere it cannot be found. Truth is in everything That Exists. Allow the Heart to feel Its Pulse, feel the winds blowing gently through the trees, and you will understand what the mind cannot comprehend. We are restructuring the imbalances brought on by this planet's constant and unending wars. Our teachings and literature are bringing vibratory balance to the elements of Light and Sound in all walks of Life, but this is only the beginning. Many participants are being secretly trained in the arts and skills that originated from lost cultures that once had dominion over this Earth. We represent a "rebirth" and "revitalization" of what once was and can be again. Our use of the secret knowledge will be used to give love where love was lost, and render balance and harmony wherever there is an open heart.

One long term vision is to have enough skilled and educated in Sugmad's army who can stand at every corner of this globe and maintain discipline, vigilance, and love in the face of darkness, so that all who seek to return to the Sea of Love and Mercy will have a clear and lighted path to follow.

This is a special time in history for The Way of Truth; there has never been a time mankind has been so close to the edge of self-destruction. The dark forces have gained unparalleled strength over the centuries due to man's spiritual laziness and refusal to accept responsibility for his actions. The fires of war are blazing on every continent; world leaders are making their decisions based on ego and the lust for power, while ignoring the plights of their peoples. There is bloodlust and mayhem everywhere, especially on this planet's Mother Africa, where citizens are routinely and systematically killed in the name of greed, ignorance and hatred – the three snakes of the Medusa. Genocide has become a way of life in these nations, and the world has largely turned its back.

Now in the great darkness of man's inhumanity to his brothers and sisters comes a path that offers hope, love and redemption, with a return to the basic teachings of the selfless, open heart. This path of the Light and Sound opens the Way for mankind to rediscover his roots in divine love, compassion, wisdom, and mercy. Humanity's Inner senses are now being awakened to greater awareness and understanding of its true place in existence, and of the powers of love within its own heart. As more Light enters humanity's consciousness, more compassion will be reflected in our physical environment. Our blessed path is an infinite source of Light and Sound and it is a vehicle by which Sugmad's Voice is expressed to touch souls throughout all time.

Heart-Opening Contemplative Exercise

1. Sit down. Relax. Take three breaths.

2. Sing the name of *"Dan Rin"* three times while holding his image with your Inner Eyes. You can also choose any spiritual teacher for whom you have an affinity.

3. Begin an Inner dialogue with the spiritual teacher via this heart-to-heart transmission

and ask whatever questions you have about your true role in this life.

4. See the words floating from your consciousness like balls of light on the beam that connects your heart to theirs.

5. Then chant this mantra: *"O-VAY-TOOM-SA-VA"* three times.

6. Stay tuned and listen for the special message of guidance that is meant only for you to receive. Or just feel the loving connection you have established with each other. Lose yourself in Joy and listen to the delicate music of the Inner Spheres.

7. End the exercise with, *"**Blessed Be**."*

8. Do this exercise for 15-30 minutes three times a week for three weeks to tap this exercise's full potential.

Humanity's Survival

A master craftsman learns his skill through diligence and careful study of the teachings of his craft. The participants of The Way of Truth must apply themselves very diligently to the teachings, discourses and heart knowledge. Participants must also work closely with the great works that are resurfacing after many centuries in seclusion. Sugmad wants Its secrets of the universe to be known to these spiritual warriors so they can teach others how to find the Light within themselves and awaken their long forgotten creativity. The writings of The Way of Truth are encoded with engrams that help stimulate the memory of skills learned in past lives that will assist mankind with its health and well-being and promote respect for the soul of planet Earth. Each participant who faithfully studies the teachings and practices the spiritual exercises can be a catalyst for growth in their fellow human beings by simply sharing what he or she knows here and there, like planting seeds that will later grow into a great harvest of brotherhood and understanding. When mankind is brought forward to a place of Self-Realization, their productivity will increase, as well as their desire to work in harmony with the natural forces of this planet.

Zadok and The Art of Manifestation

The participants who will be tutored by Master Teacher Zadok, Teacher of Jesus, will tap into the secrets of the Art of Manifestation.

This art had its origins in the lost continents of Mu, Lemuria, and Atlantis. It was taught in our mystery school and was the rite of passage for those being trained for membership in the High Priesthood. There were many droughts and famines in these ancient times. The people turned to the priests because they could manifest water and food out of the ethers; this art belongs to the Etheric Plane. The priests understood that everything in the physical world is made of rapidly moving thought particles that can be molded into materialization by strong desire and the focused application of the will. Skilled practitioners had only to envision the desired object in their Third Eyes and then call forth from the Etheric Plane the substance that would turn thought into physical reality, and it would literally drop down from the air. Jesus demonstrated this Art of Manifestation with loaves of bread and fish. This art will also turn one substance into another, as when Jesus the Christ turned water into wine.

To master this art, the practitioners must have developed their consciousness to a level above Time and Space where all reality is in a constant state of beingness. Their thoughts, driven by desire and will, instantly attract the particles from the ethers that will give it form and substance. Its heaviness drops to the Physical Plane as "out of thin air."

This is a lost art because of its misuse by those who abused a sacred trust. It is an age-old bane of mankind to fall into traps of greed and avarice. Powers like the Art of Manifestation disappear when used for self-serving purposes. They simply dry up like drops of rain on desert rocks. It can be revived in small doses by those of the highest moral fiber and consciousness when taught in secrecy within a mystery school like The Way of Truth.

The Art of Manifestation can be used for the resolution of human problems. Problems can be uncreated; we can change the energetic source of their effect.

For example, when one shoots an arrow, one can say the trajectory toward its target is inevitable. And when a problem is launched from the human condition, its trajectory also appears to be unstoppable. However, some problems can be recalled much like email being called back from cyberspace. Time is elastic and can be stretched like a rubber band. Whatever is occurring in any given point on the time-line can be called back by a shift in consciousness. The band of time can be tweaked and the problem snapped back to its source, but only if it will not interfere with any unlearned lessons for the soul or souls involved.

A problem can be uncreated if there is sincere supplication to the Holy Spirit on the part of the one experiencing it, once that person has an understanding of the spiritual laws that govern physical reality. The Law of Economy applies in this case. Once a lesson has been fully learned and absorbed into the consciousness of that soul and appears again in the form of a new problem, there is no reason to re-experience it; the band is snapped back, the email is recalled, and the problem is dissolved into the Light and Sound of God.

Soul cannot be happy unless it has a purpose in this world. Each soul was born with a written Life Contract in which it makes certain agreements with the coming incarnation. A

Life Contract is a roadmap for soul to find its way toward the completion of its goals. Within each contract there is a mission to fulfill and this is what gives soul its purpose and place in the grand scheme of life. This contract is not written to punish soul. Instead, it is soul's Emancipation Proclamation from servitude and bondage to the Lower Worlds. The Contract is designed to give soul structure and guidance as it meets the challenges of daily living. The only real happiness soul can experience is in freedom from the bonds of karma. When soul fully understands and works in harmony with the agreements of its Contract and mission, it breaks those bonds and rises to its true destiny to be in partnership with Divine Love, Joy and Bliss. The freedom of the God Worlds is a blissful state beyond the comprehension of the mind. The transitory, fleeting happiness of the human ego will not take soul beyond the Fifth Plane – it will not take it to the Realms of Wonder and True Life. A soul who is willing to carry out his or her mission with an open heart will be rewarded with more joy than he or she could possibly contain in one lifetime.

Go forward in confidence, and allow your Contract to be your greatest motivation and place of encouragement as you face the daily challenges of your life. Remember, too, that a Contract is not iron-clad, but is a living, breathing document from the heart of Sugmad. It will move and flow with the individual like a flower in a warm, summer breeze. Let it move and work with you – be alive and trust that all is working in divine, right order. You will be no stranger to

Grace on Earth and in the worlds above that wait to embrace you again.

The Cycle of Reincarnation

When we speak of reincarnation, we think of it as a solitary process in which each soul is reborn into individual lifetimes and works out his or her own karma. The ultimate truth is that all of existence is in the process of reincarnating because everything is in a state of becoming – all is moving toward greater awareness and understanding, and everything is connected.

There is not one thing in Sugmad's creation that stands apart from anything else; when one moves forward, all move forward. When one takes a giant step backward, all must stumble to one degree or another. It is like a rock climbing expedition – the group moves by individual effort, yet all are connected by the same rope. If one misses a step and falls, all are pulled backward, and they cannot continue until the one is back on solid footing.

The ultimate purpose of reincarnation is all souls' return to the Kingdom of Sugmad as God-Realized beings who take their proper place within the God Worlds to serve all of life in their own unique capacities with great joy and humility. The goal of souls' service to humanity is to bring hope where there is despair, compassion where there is tyranny, freedom where there is subjugation, and love where there is ignorance. In other words, souls' ultimate purpose is to alleviate universal suffering and promote Oneness of heart.

The cycles of reincarnation extend to all of existence, including the stars and planets. Each is moving forward in evolution. There are cycles within cycles from the evolvement of plant life to insect life to human life to the Sun and Moon and planets. The planets and all heavenly bodies have the greatest ability to move everything forward due to the emanation of strong, magnetic waves of energy, as evidenced by the Moon's influence over the tides of the mighty oceans and on human-physiological cycles. All of creation coordinates and moves in harmony with these powerful cycles of the planetary system toward the return to balance, harmony, love, truth, and wisdom.

Karmic Loops and Repetitive Cycles

Karmic loops originate from repeated behaviors that affect soul in negative ways. These behaviors are like "bad habits" that form grooves in the human consciousness and as the grooves grow deeper, they become harder to escape. It is a weakness of human nature to cling to the familiar. Even when the results cause pain, it still seems less painful to face the unknown. These habits of thinking and behavior can extend into future lifetimes presenting souls with the same situations and conditions over and over again.

The mind becomes dependent on these conditions and finds ways to re-create them repeatedly. And so, this forms what is known as a "karmic loop." Some have asked me, "Does it mean that the karma attached to the original condition is paid back repeatedly?" No, but it can be "acted out" by the mind *ad infinitum*. The mind loves drama and it also loves the familiar. Karmic loops satisfy both of these needs.

[Here Sri Michael told a story about himself and one of his professors. He kept writing papers that he thought would please the professor, who finally asked him "You don't really mean that, do you?" The professor knew the power of his heart's convictions were not behind his words. Sri Michael broke this cycle by writing what he truly believed. As a result, he was rewarded with a much higher grade.]

A "repetitive cycle" does not necessarily have to be a "karmic loop." A repetitive cycle does not always contain elements of karma. It can be the choosing of same type of mate over and over again, or it can be harmful eating habits, or repeating the same behavior at work that causes one to be dismissed, and so forth.

Breaking the Cycle

Karmic loops can be broken by changing one's thought patterns and behavior step by step. I like to use "thought-substitution" which is to exchange one word or image for another. Do this technique each time a dark thought enters your mind and you will train it to "jump the groove" and move on to the next song on the album of your life.

Another way to break a repetitive cycle is to make small, gradual changes in your daily routine. Get up a half hour earlier, sit in a different chair than usual, take a walk instead of watching TV at the regular time. Read literature that expands your awareness instead of the same old mystery novels that you love to indulge in. Anything that takes a departure from the norm will pull you out of the circular trenches of your mentality and back onto the open roads of your highest life!

The Origin of the HU Life Code

There are many Sugmads and many universes; each universe has its own divine signature. The Father of All That Is assigns a life code that is unique to the structure of each universe, and unique to their goals and life forms. The "HU" was chosen for this Sugmad because of its ability to harmonize with the blueprints of Its vision and purpose for this magnificent undertaking – Its worlds upon worlds of creation. Each plane of reality and all its inhabitants are connected to Sugmad by Its own singular sound vibration. This is what distinguishes one universe from another and one evolutionary group of souls from another. HU is the unifying force of the domain of this Sugmad and is the sound that will lead all to find their true home in the Sea of Love and Mercy. It was given to soul as a gift of freedom that will unlock every door to every plane of existence, and is also a "homing device" that keeps soul from straying into the dark abyss of the lower realms of Kal's hierarchies.

The HU was designed to give every sentient being their own key to Heaven and to unlock the truth within them. No universal structure can exist without its own system of life principles. We have HU because it is the sound by which our Sugmad relates to the One Father. Like a human parent gives their child a name, so was this Sugmad given a unique sound by Its Father to distinguish It from Its Brothers and Sisters. HU is the sound by which our Sugmad is known to Its Father. That sound carries the life code of All That Is in our universe.

What is True, Real and Spiritually Valuable

Since primitive times, man has always been drawn to others of like mind and feeling – this was crucial to his survival in very dangerous and hostile environments. These early groups formed families and villages, and learned to adapt to the harsh world around them by creating rituals and a belief system they could rely on for help and protection. This system of beliefs included worship of the elements and of the unseen forces around them. They wore amulets, built altars, made animal sacrifices, chanted, danced and prayed. Thus, religion was created as a method of survival in those early times.

Over the centuries, religion has become the grounding force that connects humanity to the natural and supernatural world and to the divine love and protection it sought. No society can stand without a system of beliefs and no people can survive for long without a code of ethics. All would fall into chaos within a very short time without these pillars of strength to hold up the foundation of each culture.

How these belief systems and morals define what people consider to be true and spiritually valuable

Belief systems have stood the test of time and have been handed down from generation to generation. People willingly accept the ideology of those in positions of authority - from parents to priests to world and church leaders. The older a belief and the longer it has existed, the more power it is given in the human consciousness. Such long held beliefs do not need to be proven to seem real.

How this perspective places a threshold around the individual consciousness in each culture

Long held beliefs limit the imagination and man's ability to think for himself. Humanity has been largely in a "sleep state" – there have always been more followers than leaders. Those who dared to think "outside the box" were rewarded with persecution and death. It is easier, safer and more comfortable to go along with the crowd. And so, we have what is known as the "collective consciousness" of man. Falling into step with this group agreement limits how far one can travel on his or her own, and places imaginary boundaries around the heart of one's creativity. You can step across the threshold by going within in contemplation and listening minutely to the subtle but powerful guidance of the heart. Regular communion with the Inner self is what will break the bonds of conformity and conduct, and open the door to higher awareness, freedom of expression, Self-Realization and ultimately God-Realization. Be who you truly are and create "outside the box" and some part of our world will change toward its highest and greatest good.

The Five Keys of Spiritual Wisdom

The *first* and most important key is love; we must be able to distinguish from the love which is divine and that of personal affection. It will come down to the individual to decide whether they are being motivated by Sugmad's Will or their own.

The *second* is service: it can be a divine calling, or giving your time to the spreading of The Way of Truth's works in accordance with your individual choice, but 'service' is also serving your family and raising your children at home. Your heart must lead you in the second key.

The *third* key is to surrender all attachments and let go of the grip of ego. In doing so we are releasing the spiritual tension behind our actions and are acting in the best interests of all concerned.

The *fourth* key is having faith and developing the open heart. Building one's stamina to face our daily challenges creates a knowingness that Sugmad loves us no matter what error or grievous mistake we make.

The *fifth* key is wisdom and honor, and this is performing our daily tasks and duties with trust, loyalty and devotion. This is what America's young people are doing in Iraq, serving the U.S. Armed Services in our attempt to bring peace to a 2,000 year karmic cycle between Judaic, Christian, and Islamic cultures.

Love is the first spiritual key of wisdom because there is no wisdom without love. Everything in life moves in the direction of love; love is the reason we are here. We gather experiences in our quest for Love, and through these experiences we grow in spirit and garner the fruits of wisdom.

Love and Blessings to each of you in your journey home.

~ Sri Michael

Module Four:

2008 Sehaji Transcripts

The Way of Truth Universal Retreat

Baltimore, Maryland

October 23 - 26, 2008

I want to thank each of you for coming to our Blessed Retreat. There are some who have traveled quite far to be with us today. Since theology's beginnings, man and womankind have gathered together like this to honor the workings of the Light and Sound of God.

Before we begin to travel the depths of prophecy, I want to touch on the subject of experiences to expect beyond the Seventh Circle of Initiation and this upcoming Presidential Election.

We stand at a turning point in American history. At no time in American history have women gained such prominence in the Democratic and Republican Parties and no one of color has ever gone this far in a Presidential Race.

This Presidential Race will decide the outcome of the next hundred years of Earth's history and will have a direct effect on our distant cousins from other star systems and how they will reveal themselves to mankind.

The rate of Earth's ecosystem and environmental changes will accelerate and thereby create weather anomalies and catastrophes which will directly affect the development and industrial growth of various countries in the Far East,

America's coastal regions and areas of Europe, which for centuries experienced no real weather problems.

The disconnection many participants are feeling has to do with the Silent Nine holding the flow of the Light and Sound to adjust the Earth's vibratory rate to accommodate the changes forthcoming after the Presidential Race. Had this not occurred the manifestation of fear and anger surfacing before the election would have escalated in violence and political catastrophes, to include assassination of individuals being trained in Shambala and in the spiritual city of Agam Des.

Today, October 25, 2008, represents the day the Vatican historical staff presents the original manuscript of the Templar Order being tried by Philip the Fair in the late Thirteenth Century. It vindicates the Templars of the false charges of heresy and Vatican records officially reflect the misdeeds exacted on them on this very day.

■■

The presence of Hilary Clinton and Sarah Palin reveals the successful efforts of the female Sehaji Masters insuring that women will be playing an important role in world politics. It is also important to note that the female political and social leaders who will emerge will represent often different views from our own; some will be ultra-conservative right wing and some will be extremely liberal. All categories of life will have symbolic and meaningful representation - without it there would be no democracy.

It should be noted for those of higher initiations beyond the Seventh Circle, it should be expected that conscious expansion of awareness will take various forms of experience, because you are being trained not to rely on physical reality as the entirety of your perceptions. The Inner Master's Presence, which is the light form of the Living Sehaji Master, will not be holding your hand once you have been given entry into the neophyte - beginning levels - of God-Realization. To be given the gifts that go with these Circles, you must be vigilant in committed service, faith and knowingness that the Light and Sound is a facet of every momentary event in your life. The gifts and awareness work and coincide with the service to the mission God has given to The Way of Truth and to your soul agreement to serve humanity. One of the gifts that coincide with the Eighth Circle is the ability to control the weather. One of my teachers, Tom Flamma, the first member of the Eighth Circle in America, used this gift of "changing weather" very wisely, but he had a need for it. The gifts come with how you serve with an open heart with no expectations, and if your service requires the need of it.

I went five years without a single experience or intuitive nudge from any of my previous teachers. I went with the confirmation and knowingness that what I had been given prior to this period was an opportunity and gift. This period allowed me to see clearly the gift of having life itself, of having a healthy body, of having good friends and family that loved me. You will be given the void-like experience of an emptiness and disconnection; much like the self-induced purification of St. John's and Jesus' in the desert. How can the God Worlds absorb your consciousness into Its Infinite Purity, if it is not allowed to empty the cup of your prior experiences? It cannot thereby fill it with heavenly bliss and God-Awareness. To be in God Consciousness we will be called upon to empty everything and surrender; and gain universal knowingness. For further elaboration on what has been mentioned, read Chapter Three in *Paramitas, the Gathering of Many Rivers*, entitled "The Silent Journey Within." Especially read and study the second paragraph on page 47. One of my most notable spiritual experiences was a period of six months in emptiness, the feeling of disconnection and devout silence. Periods and cycles of this nature can be used to consciously create, to send thoughts of goodwill and healing to affect not only the present, but the past and future as well. One can literally go into the past and change its course with a thought projected from a highly-charged, concentrated and focused act of will. Negativity dissipates in the presence of positive thoughts and meaningful, open-hearted detached goodwill.

The art of seeing past and present is a gift and talent that exceeds the age of this planet. There are beings who move by thought projection and arcs of light that fold time and space and use this art for scientific research. They have a highly developed Mental Body and can be seen at the periphery of our vision. Their Physical Bodies are like flashes and short lines of light.

The true sight of prophetic vision allows the seer to understand the root cause of what they "see." Seeing can be an "Inner movement" that later comes to the seer like a holographic thought form or what one would typify as a "mind-picture." It is similar to watching an old movie reel's flashing frames inside your head.

There are three degrees of prophecy:

The *first degree of prophecy* is the ability to change the present by going back in time to change the present without disturbing karmic balances. It is the act of going back to a past action and reference point of energy and changing the resonance of the signal it is sending in the present. I knew of a participant who had continually revolving problems around the men she chose for relationships. She was affected by a comment her parent said of her being stupid and would not amount to much in life. This single comment made to a child before puberty emanated a signal of unworthiness and made her an emotional target for abusive partners. She was given the spiritual materials in the chapter on "The Nature of Loving Relationships" in *The Discovery of Self*. This participant's serious commitment to this study and her use of the two techniques revealed the incident of her parent's comment; it was buried under a heap of emotional obstacles she had forgotten in the incident. She started to realize that she was taking a different stance on her present-potential relationships. She decided to make a list of characteristics she wanted in her mate and would not compromise on what she wanted. Within the scope of two years she released her feelings of inadequacy and married a man of professional means who nurtures her every need. This gift of prophecy changes the vibration of a present problem or challenge. It dissipates the magnetic hold a situation has on you. You can use the spiritual exercise at the end of the chapter "Prophesy: The Art of Seeing beyond the Veil" in *Paramitas* to gain understanding and use of this gift. There is a hidden component that the Inner Master must give you to gain complete use of the degree of prophesy, but even partial use of it can create a miracle. There are volumes of literature associated with this gift; greatness of soul can come with diligent study.

The *second degree of prophecy* consists of seeing an event coming within moments of its occurrence. The seer who has this ability must take extra care in discretion, discrimination and interpretation. There is a multitude of events coming into simultaneous manifestation. The seer must identify and separate the specific frequency of Light and Sound from the other events that are coming into their focus. Imagine several different scenes on a television screen; you have pulled out the specific event you are looking at and have dragged and dropped it on a separate scene in your Middle Eye. If you tune in on the event at the earlier stage it begins to emanate a spiritual signal; you could literally change the event and/or nip it from existing. This seer often works with the Lords of Karma and other select spiritual masters who have duties maintaining this planet's Soul Contract.

The *third degree of prophecy* is the ability to see major planetary changes and the ability to know the arrival of those souls who would have a significant impact on world history. This seer is in contact with beings not of this Earth and can use its Mental Body to physically travel through space, folding Light and time. This seer can be used as an intermediary between humanity and extraterrestrials who are requesting specific exchanges for their research and scientific growth. The spiritual master Rumi interacts with the higher forms of these races. They maintain a refined Thought Body and soul. They have supervisory control of the other ET life forms. The life forms described by Paul Twitchell's writings have come into formal agreements to adhere to the Life Contract of this planet. Their intent is to examine our development of human will and to use vital resources on Earth our sciences have yet to discover and use. This *seer must also work wit*h Shamus-I-Tabriz and Sat Nam to review the Soul Records of those who have agreed to take the responsibility of world leadership. In their sight is the healing power of "Theta."

Theta is a light source filtered by the Third Eye and is a healing technique of the Brown Robe Mastership of the Physical Worlds. This technique was effectively used by such spiritual giants as Jesus, Nicolas of Myra, and Sri Yukteswar. Somewhere within the two books *Paramitas* and *The Discovery of Self* this power is further examined and discussed. The Druids used stones as conduits of Light and Sound to use "Theta" and it is a gift awaiting some souls who establish themselves in the Court of Sat Nam. Key aspects of

"Theta" are the mantras, words of making and a refinement of heart and the Third Eye. They must be used in combination and its use is monitored by the masters of Agam Des and Shambala.

America, the Land of the Free

Balance is the key word to progress in the United States of America. Things here have been leaning too far in one extreme or its opposite. There has been no one driving this runaway locomotive in the last 50 years. Eisenhower was the last true leader of this country who had a grasp of the middle group. He understood that people are easily led into anarchy and chaos because of the extreme instability and excitability of the human Emotional Body. We are seeing excitability in today's Political Race. The way to find balance in this country and to preserve its sacred sovereignty is for each citizen to have no opinions, but to have convictions. What is the truth that speaks to your heart? What is the feeling of "rightness" in the daily decisions each person must make? Balance is simply following what seems right in any given moment. Each human is guided ultimately by soul and soul knows all. Nobody is "truly lost" or without guidance in this life. Humanity was programmed to be consistently "in-touch" with the Higher Powers that oversee this universe.

There is no such thing truly as a "lost soul," even though it may seem to be a reality for some individuals who have fallen off the moral and spiritual path. The reality is that each and every soul created by Sugmad has a homing device that keeps it ever in tune with the guidance of its highest aspect, soul, and of The Creator. It can never go wrong if it simply follows the "Inner calling," the nudges and feelings of right or wrong. Every animal known to man ultimately and truly knows that they have done or are doing something wrong. They do it anyway because they are driven by imbalance of thought and feeling. Every wrong action or choice builds upon itself until it becomes a driving force that runs amok in the human Emotional and Mental Bodies. The way to bring it back is often through a source of intervention such as illness, accident or some misfortune that guides the attention of the individual back to reason, understanding, forgiveness and love. Sugmad, also known as God, will not let a runaway train go off the track and destroy life. It will stop the train through Divine intervention and set it straight once again. This is a law of life, no one will be allowed to ultimately destroy the plans Sugmad has set in motion. That is the only unstoppable force in this world - the Eternal Will of God.

The Presidential Election

Obama is the engineer that Sugmad has chosen to get the train called America on its track to freedom, sovereignty, prosperity and overall balance. He has also been chosen as an ambassador of race equality and unity and to remove the lines of racial division that have plagued the Earth for many centuries. He is a mixture of Black and White heritage, which is symbolic of his mission to unite the races. John

McCain represents the old forces that have kept America stagnant and bound by limited, provincial and fearful thinking. His entire campaign has excited the instability of the lowest of emotions in the human body. Change is truly the underlying element of this election, but it goes deeper than economics, politics and religion; it is the change from darkness to light in the human consciousness. Nothing can move or change on this Earth without individual effort; it all begins with each human being who can make the choice of right and wrong in their own heart. They cannot make these choices amid the chaos of fearful chants and shouts from within themselves, which is then amplified one hundred fold in the outside world. McCain is a former war hero and a noble soul, but he has been blindsided by fear and ambition. He is not a true statesman who can see both sides of an issue with fairness and calm deliberation, because he cannot hear the voice of reason above the shouts from his own consciousness and from those around him who reflect and magnify that fear. This political election is pivotal to the regaining of the American Spirit, which is of the people, by the people and for the people. Each person has a voice that must be heard and a heart that must be followed. America is now ready for a leader who can be in touch with the spirit of the people without fear or repression of the truth, and who can overcome social lines of division and re-establish the seeds of unity and freedom that are the spiritual foundation of this great country.

Let us move toward the consciousness of balance. The re-emergence of the feminine energies in this physical world of manifestation will replenish, rejuvenate, nurture, and balance the Earth's consciousness. As women gain strength and acceptance in positions of political leadership, their nurturing and life giving influence will reach into the fields of science, medicine, astronomy, metaphysics and all educational fields of study. It is so far reaching as to be incomprehensible to the current state of human understanding. The women operating behind the scenes of the Democratic Ticket, as well as in its forefront, represent the highest potential of the feminine influence for good in this world. They have the qualities of keen intelligence, strength of character, and a firm grasp of the masculine fortitude necessary to overcome the inherent weakness that is normally attributed to the "weaker sex." These women are opening the doors of opportunity for women in the Republican Party, which is still dealing with the spiritual vibration and old chauvinism that says women should be "seen and not heard." There will be more than one female President forthcoming in the next forty years. Sugmad is re-balancing this Earth and the universe at large away from the dominant male drive to conquer and divide, control and destroy; and bring it back to a verdant green and flowering garden that sustains all life, love and liberty. Women have the ability to create life through their connection to the God States and they will be the major players to bring new life back to the Earth and its inhabitants. This is what is upholding the great changes and is representative of Sugmad's plans to balance our planet Earth.

Our collective Free Will guides the course of this planet and sets the destiny of 2012 to 2112 and prophetic events within this historic period of one hundred years.

Forecast of Future Events

A greater focus on the economy, Social Security and medical benefits will energetically release a floodgate of new music and arts. This artistic awareness will bring a positive revitalization of goodwill and love throughout the world.

A famine and/or plague is awaiting the Middle East if the Iraqi War continues. Negativity is collecting in one area and over time will vibrationally affect what comes from the ground. The one plant unaffected will be the poppy plant and the drug trade will flourish, along with arms purchases from weapons brokers from the U.S., the Soviet Union and China.

The Light and Sound frequencies of the Mental Plane are opening the door of the Soul Plane for those souls who are spiritually awake. Many open hearted souls who are simply giving service in the capacity given to them will have the opportunity of gaining Soul Consciousness. This will mean a greater scope of awareness beyond the concrete world will open their Third Eyes to see what is currently being veiled from them by life forms not of this Earth. In essence, there will be more sightings of crafts, physical manipulations, abductions and extraterrestrials walking this Earth. The books *Discovery of Self* and *Paramitas* will give many aspirants the opportunity of gaining entry into the spiritual city of Agam Des, Shamballa and Nampak.

What can heal this planet and set a course for greater planetary stability will be humanity's decision to be and stay in the Heart Consciousness. It is Love's greatest conduit and creates an infectious environment of Free Will.

For the artists in all of us, close your eyes and I will read you this poem:

> *"I am the beginning and essence of Eternity*
> *Through me is offered that which is Absolute Truth*
> *In my arts is an expression of Spirit's works*
> *Is found the purest love of Sugmad."*

Mantra: "I see, I feel and I am this Love" *("TOMPI-TU-HU-SA-SE.")*

Nicholas of Myra – C. 342

Nicholas was a highly revered Catholic Saint who lived in the Third Century. He was twenty-five years old when Gabriel approached him while he was working in the garden of his mother's home.

Gabriel appeared as a dancing spark of light in the dandelions. Nicholas thought this apparition was some type of moth or butterfly and thus began a metamorphosis from this speck of light to a full form and substance of the

Archangel Gabriel. There was a halo of golden light around his head and shoulders. Thus, began Nicholas' training under the tutelage of Gabriel. Nicholas was chosen to be the Patron Saint of the Lost and Homeless. Gabriel gave Nicholas the key to a great many gifts, one of which was the ability to break up the past residue of karma and lift it from the person. He worked the streets, uplifting hearts, and healed the sick with the gifts of the Lavender Robe Order. He would resurrect a select number of people who died during the December time frame. In later times, he became known as St. Nicholas, opening the creation of the modern day Santa Claus.

Nicholas learned resurrection during a prior lifetime studying under Sehaji Master Gopal Das in the Temple of Ra. He knew how to reconnect the Silver Cord of those who had died and were still lingering close by. Some participants present here knew him and worked with him during this period of time. Before Nicholas reincarnated into the Third Century his prior lifetime was during the Roman Occupation of Jerusalem. He was a mentor to Jesus and taught him the gift of resurrection. Nicholas in Soul Body was standing next to Jesus when he resurrected Lazarus and called him forth from his tomb. Such gifts are given through "thought-transference" of the Mental Bodies. In essence, the only action Nicholas had to take was to keep his heart completely open and simply sat across from his Teacher and absorb his knowledge through a secret method that will one day be available to select members of humanity.

When Nicholas spoke to the hearts of others he would say, "I am ready to give away the gift of love in my heart to whomever is ready to receive it."

He wanted his students to treat the heart as a gift to others.

The Discovery of Self

Taking individual responsibility for the thoughts, words and deeds that each person expresses on a daily basis is the underlying foundation for peace, democracy and a better world for all living souls on this Earth. It is really that simple. The mess America is in is so far out of control that is doesn't matter what the experts have to say on the economy, the infrastructure and the political situation. They can argue and analyze it to death, but seen from the higher perspective of this world and a universal view, and from the viewpoint of soul, none of this analysis or problem solving carries any weight or can make any difference. The most wise, most learnt and most knowledgeable amongst us cannot alone and/or by themselves, undo the mess this country is in. But the simplest thought from an average person can start the ball rolling towards recovery and sanity, sense and democracy, liberation and new ground. That thought should be "I AM." I will repeat "I AM." Then say: "**I AM LOVE**," then say "**I AM PEACE**" and thereafter say "**I AM WITH GOD'S LOVE, I AM ONE WITH GOD'S PEACE**." Take this posture and exercise to the election campaigns and to the White House and to the League of Nations. Take this home. Take this to work. Take this to school. Take this to the market. Take this to bed.

There is nothing absolutely that exists outside the realm of LOVE and nothing can be fixed outside the realm of love and brotherhood. The political race between Barak Obama and John McCain is showing the light and dark sides of human nature. Sugmad is tired of watching man's hatred, ignorance, and inhumanity towards his brethren. And so he sent one who could stoke up the olde ways of thinking and behaving. Sugmad said, "It is time for a Black world leader and I want him planted in America. I want all of the weeds of intolerance to be blighted out by the growth of brotherly love and tolerance. I want to ask the people to honor the dignity and divinity of their humanity and become blind to color and race barriers. There are no barriers or divisions in Sugmad's kingdom and those who will not recognize the basic divinity and dignity of their fellow human beings shall not be allowed into the God Worlds until they reach full maturity; such is the purpose of reincarnation."

As Jesus, Zoroastar, Babaji and many other great spiritual masters have said, "Love one another" to countless souls who were lost in fear and ignorance. They did not mean; "Love ye only those who are like yourself." He meant "Love the love in your brother's and sister's hearts." Fearful ignorance has been the bane of this world for many thousands of years. It starts in the mind as a thought, which generates a feeling, which generates an action. Let Love be the choice in your thoughts now; it is the only way to salvation in these very turbulent and critical times.

Keeping the World in Balance

To the participants who see their missions as to keeping select elite groups from buying up the world's stock markets and taking over this planets destiny, I recommend the following:

I would like to see each participant of The Way of Truth connect and energetically learn the high ground with a mentor and spiritual master of their choice; for this is a mission that cannot be done alone. If your mission entails taking on the dark forces of this world and their channels, the guidance and protection of a highly advanced master is required. So the first thing I advise is for each participant to go into contemplation and ask for or choose a spiritual master to be your mentor. Simply focus on the Spiritual Eye in your forehead and say, "I want to help. I humbly call forth a master of the Holy Order of Spiritual Masters." Or you can choose a master as a mentor by chanting "HU" three times and then chanting their name three times while picturing them in your Spiritual Eye. If you cannot envision their face, see their name before you. Once you have made contact with your mentor, you can meet them in contemplation and ask how you can help to shape and preserve the destiny of this world.

For the warriors of The Way of Truth, these times are the most exciting and spiritually challenging times in human history. The opportunity for spiritual advancement is unprecedented and unlimited.

The Expansion of Awareness

This area of focus comes from page 100 of *The Discovery of Self*. The expansion of awareness will cause a period of physical restlessness and some agitation in the Physical Body during periods of prayer, contemplation and during your day. What is happening is a rising shift of spiritual energy inside you. Just begin to observe yourself closely. This increase in thought is often labeled as boredom, nervousness or the inability to "sit still" or "get it." But what is actually happening is the higher energies of soul expansion and awareness are powering in and thereby opening new reference points of energy inside of you. Instead of getting up, this is precisely the time to remain still and simply go deep inside with open receptivity and growing awareness and a resolve to gain and retain what you are receiving.

The mind and physical bodies were built to hold and be a receptacle for the God energy. You can actually warehouse a great deal of spiritual energy and knowledge without any mental understanding of it.

Use the contemplative prayer song in *Discovery of Self* on page 129 for inspiration. Read it aloud to yourself after singing three "*HU's*."

You are being asked to differentiate between the discomfort of change from what the mind is trying to identify as an alarm for fear. Just declare yourself to be a vehicle for God's love; and just devote your time to the truths imparted to your heart. Do not fear change; grow into Higher Realms with your spiritual master and Inner Master at your side.

Let us try out the contemplative exercise on page 101:

Contemplative Prayer to Communicate with Sugmad

1. Start by singing the Life Code for this Sugmad *"HU"* six times.

2. Chant *"DAN RIN"* seven times.

3. Imagine a purifying golden light penetrating the heart center and burning all impurities completely. Feel the lightness.

4. Chant the mantra *"SU-KI-LE"* (Soo-key-lay) for 5-10 minutes and see electric waves coming from Sugmad's heart to the center of your heart. You feel a little jolt in your heart, you feel your whole being heating up; love fills your heart; every cell of your body becomes alive and vibrates. Sugmad is communicating with you.

5. Listen to your heart and see what Sugmad has to tell you. Ask It to give you Its view of what is being conveyed in the workshops; your spiritual conversations and in the two sessions regarding Prophecy and *The Discovery of Self.*

6. End the exercise with, "Blessed Be."

Stories to Share

St. Jerome of the Fourth Century was instrumental in keeping the linguistic integrity of the Bible's translation. He spent the greater course of his life delving into its interpretation. The course of his enlightenment was entrenched with Angelic visions and visitations; he was trained spiritually by Gabriel to capture Jesus' heart and teachings of the Light and Sound. Jerome had the ability to read and see the "past events" around Jesus and the disciples through the magnetic resonance left on grounds they traveled and sanctified. He could collapse "time and space" as described by past masters of the Sehaji to witness historic events of the past. Jerome was one of Nostradamus' spiritual mentors and taught him the more advanced levels of prophetic vision.

Various members of female Roman nobility protected Jerome from physical harm and provided him with the economic resources to achieve his spiritual mission. He inspired women of nobility to form ascetic monasteries and always felt they were closer to the heart of God. This closeness was created by their ability to "let go" and let love be their guide in all things. Jerome foresaw today's political climate and also saw changes within other theological institutions.

Let us use the Contemplative Prayer song from page 129 of *The Discovery of Self – First Edition.*

St. Jerome's Contemplative Exercise

Pain and disappointment are machinations of the mind to test the mettle of soul; they are wisps of clouds attempting to obscure the rays of the sun. They can be easily blown away in a single breath of faith and resolve!

1. The next time clouds begin to weight heavy in your heart and mind, sing *"HU"* three times and say this out loud to them: *"GO AWAY. YOU DO NOT EXIST. MY SKY IS OPEN AND CLEAR. MY HEART IS FREE. SO LEAVE IN THE NAME OF THE MOST HOLY. I DO NOT RECOGNIZE YOU. "*

2. You may also simplify this into a postulate: *"MY SKY IS OPEN AND DEAR. MY HEART IS FREE."*

3. Then imagine the clouds of pain and disappointment disappearing from your sky until it is clear and blue again. It is that simple.

Blessed Be.

~ Sri Michael

Module Five:

The Book
of
The Beginning

THE WAY OF TRUTH

The Book

of

The Beginning

Michael Edward Owens

OPEN HEART BOOKS

Copyright © 2005 by Michael Edward Owens. All rights reserved.

No part of this book may be reproduced by any mechanical, photographic, or electronic process, or in the form of a phonographic recording; nor may it be stored in a retrieval system, transmitted, or otherwise be copied for public or private use - other than for "fair use" as brief quotations embodied in articles and reviews without prior written permission of the publisher.

The authors of this book do not dispense medical advice or prescribe the use of any techniques as forms of treatment for physical or medical problems without the advice of a physician, either directly or indirectly. The intent of the author is only to offer information of a general nature to help you in your quest for emotional and spiritual well-being. In the event you use any of the information in this book for yourself, which is your constitutional right, the author and the publisher assumes no responsibility for your actions.

First printing May 2005
Second printing May 2008
Third printing January 2009
Fourth printing January 2010
Fifth printing October 2011

~Table of Contents~

~ Introduction ~

Yours is a mission of great merit. I, Babaji, an acknowledged Master in the way of the Light and Sound, say to you that you have opened the consciousness of many Souls to this new beginning. I offer my assistance and blessings to this journey in all ways. As before, in my journeys as a Master to many others that have brought the message of love to the hearts of those that sought to feel the presence of God on this Earth, I have laid down a foundation of spiritual interest that has been hidden from the hearts of many, but once again is being felt in this universe.

The key for this compelling process of enlightenment is that the Light and Sound in this universe has gained a new strength. It has been felt in many of the Higher Realms of Beingness as you in The Way of Truth have changed the frequency to make it more available to all souls that are being awakened in your efforts to please this Sugmad. The souls that have flocked to the entrances of these new vortices of spiritual energy will truly find the beginning that has no end.

~ Babaji

~ Level One ~

The Way of Truth

Defining The Way of Truth

Sri Tremulen:

Welcome. You have just taken a step that will enlarge your perspective of this universe to allow you to see and understand things that have perplexed you in this life and many other lifetimes that you will soon be made aware of as you walk the path of open consciousness that The Way of Truth presents to those who have been brought to this time in their hearts. At some time in your life, you have been spoken to by a voice from a place that you only sensed but never experienced in your waking moments. This voice is one that is seemingly familiar to you, as though you have heard it many times before, but in this moment it has awakened in you the need and desire to follow it to its origin. The Way of Truth is a doorway that has been placed for those who have a feeling of a great purpose to this existence and to the things that you experience in everyday living. You have been brought to this moment by beings in this universe who know more of who you are than you know yourself. This sense of knowing has presented itself as a mystery to you in a dream and conversations with others who have been touched by this universal hand of awakening. The Way of Truth has been placed in your consciousness for the sake of answering these questions and more that have been shadows in your mind. To walk this path will take a commitment of heart that will only broaden the vision of this universe and open a new view of an Inner life that has been unseen for the reason that there has never been a light shown upon it.

Once you have seen the Jewel of the Heart through the open eyes of a true seeker of understanding that has been awakened in you, your quest for wisdom and truth will carry you to worlds of wonder and fulfillment that you may have suspected were a part of a life you once lived before. The sound of HU will help in opening your consciousness to the nesting place of awareness that you are about to step into. Sing this word, HU, as a love song to God, in asking for the fulfillment that your heart tells you is yours to have once you act on the desires that have lain dormant in you until this moment.

The Way of Truth is a Mystery School

To lift a veil that clouded the vision is to see that what you have been experiencing is only a pale representation of the truth and will provoke in you one simple question: Why? The Way of Truth will help answer this question as it takes you through the mysteries of beingness in a vast, new universe that is about to open to you. Thoughts, new ideas and visions within your dreams will be some of the many ways that those who have been in your life as unseen mentors will make their presences known to you. The idea of a mystery school is a part of time immemorial and has been part of the conclusions drawn by many great philosophers who exist as teachers in the unseen realms of being. Their effort to unravel the keys to understanding the infinite soul in the universe is the legacy left behind in many hidden writings enmeshed with clues, which leave only more unanswered questions to the student of Life.

The Way of Truth guides you to your true self and a consciousness of being that allows that self to gain understanding of the Inner workings of the universe within each one of you. This is a universe, which, until this time, has been a mystery to the hearts and minds of many people. Until now, it has been shrouded in less than exact terms of understanding, but through the teachings of The Way of Truth, the heart is opened to what is called the Light and Sound, which is the true fabric of being in this universe.

As a student of this Mystery School, you will find that the true questions are not "why" but "how" do you become an active part of this unfoldment in this universe of love. There have been openings to this path through other ways of life, but those have let the true definition of being (the Light and Sound) dissipate to become only a concept and not the experience that will be found in The Way of Truth, for in these teachings given by the Living Master of the Light and Sound is found the love that God has intended us all to share as we journey back to our beginnings in the Heart of God (that we chose to call Sugmad.)

The Origin of The Way of Truth as the New Path of the Light and Sound is Ageless

The Way of Truth has always been in existence, but until this time it had been held in the shadows of the egos of those who would not let it be shared as Sugmad desired. Through this universe there is an energy that has been described in many ways - as universal, cosmic, divine, etc., but its true origin is in the Light and Sound of Sugmad's existence. The Way of Truth, through the process of initiation, has opened the hearts of many travelers seeking to once again be comforted in the Heart of God by this great Light and Sound and to share the bounty of Sugmad's love with all existence.

This has always been the wish of this universe, to share the vision of Oneness in Love with all its inhabitants. This is the purpose of the experience of being. Therefore, the beings of great wisdom who performed the duties of creation in this universe stored the true concept of the Light and Sound in a teaching to be shared at this time as The Way of Truth. It is here to help soul return to its home in the center of creation, the Heart of Sugmad.

The Present Leader and Teacher of The Way of Truth and How he Obtained His Position

The masters of this universe knew that at this time there would have to be a conduit to re-establish the true balance of the Light and Sound to insure that this universe would take its place according to the wishes of Sugmad. They set forth a task of great importance that required someone well-trained in the arts of prophecy and Universal Soul Movement to bring out their message of love and communion as presented in The Way of Truth. Only a person who had seen everything from all conceivable aspects of action, experience, and beingness could stand up to the training necessary to bring about this new path for the Light and Sound. Once chosen, this individual was observed in all things, good and bad, and allowed to make every conceivable mistake as he searched for his true self and, once exhausted by this training, was given the opportunity to change and increase the frequency of the Light and Sound in this time of Sugmad's plan. His name was given as Dan Rin, and when the offer was made to him, he asked why and was told, "You've made every possible mistake, so you are completely ready to give of yourself in the unattached way of a true master of the Light and Sound."

After past holders of the Light and Sound took their preconceived steps to try and hold the love of God from all that sought it, those who oversee the workings of the universe passed the Rod of Power to Dan Rin to re-ignite the fire of truth in the Light and Sound. All the masters who had come before, and even those yet to be, stepped forward to usher in this new time of Love and Light brought by Sri Michael Owens to the consciousness of the Sehaji, who had prepared him from time before the beginning and through many lifetimes to be this holder of the Mantle of the Rod of Power and the keeper of the new Light and Sound.

How Sri Michael Owens Descended from an Unbroken Line of Masters that Exceeds the Age of Planet Earth

In the teachings that have been passed from master to master through time far before this universe came into existence, the power of Sugmad's love transmitted through the Light and Sound was shared amongst those of pure hearts and understanding. These masters carry with them the signature of Sugmad's Grace in the form of great compassion for all entities of beingness in all realms of existence and through the universes in the Heart of all Sugmads. This cloak of sight can only be felt and initiated by the great overseers of time itself. Only those brought forward by this Council of great beings can be given the duty to guide all souls toward the true Heart of Being. Sri Michael Owens has been brought into action by the needs of the Great Ones to have this universe guided to join those that have gone before and those to come after, to celebrate the love of Sugmad in all inhabitants of Its Heart.

All the forces that balance every area of all that is known to represent life have come to join with Sri Michael to raise the Light and Sound to what can only be described as the Renaissance of Life to bring the God Realms closer to the Worlds of Duality so that all may touch the vibration of joy felt in the Great Sea of Love and Mercy. In this is the foundation of The Way of Truth.

Why The Way of Truth is Unique and Different from Other Ways of Life

The Way of Truth shines as the light of dedication of the Templar and Grail Knights who swore to maintain the purity of the teachings of the Light and Sound in the times of darkness on this planet. The Way of Truth has the duty of increasing the frequency of the love in this universe and preserving the Light and Sound in all ways of life and teachings. This aspiration brings the center of Sugmad's love to the hearts of all beings in all universes to the awareness of love throughout all time. This is the intensity of purpose that has been handed down by the Oversouls of time and existence for The Way of Truth to be reborn in the hearts of all that seek the love of God in all actions that transpire in life. The Light and Sound is the foundation for all seekers of truth from every way of life to show the love of God and to carry the knowingness that there can never be an end to this love.

Sri Michael's Mission and the Role The Way of Truth Plays in It

As the action of a people in a given realm can reflect the need for balance throughout the entire universe, so has the mission of The Way of Truth on this planet been ordained. The release of a great people from the bonds of the dark forces on this planet was the awakening of Sugmad's Fire in this universe. As Sri Michael sets about to change the karmic contract of these peoples with the help of all the forces in this Sugmad (which until now had not been done), this in turn releases into the Heart of Being across all realms of existence a reconnection to the power of compassion and love.

The Way of Truth is the focusing lens for the new frequency in this and many other universes for many other types of beings yet unknown to the consciousness of people here and in other realms. As the initiates of The Way of Truth move closer to the Heart of Sugmad and lose their cloak of illusion, the vibration of the Light and Sound is increased and spreads to reach those who still labor in the worlds of illusion and pain.

The Sehaji Masters and How They Assist Sri Michael and the Participants of the Revitalized Path of the Light and Sound

Until this time, the limitations on the Living Master of the Light and Sound had prevented the great change that is taking place. The Sehaji are an order of Oversouls (masters) that govern the evolution of all Souls in their journey to the Heart of Creation in all universes. They are superordinate to, but include within their number the Detached Masters, whose influence is restricted to this universe. This higher order of masters has come forward as the number of souls being carried into the Light and Sound need guidance. It is the guidance that only Dan Rin (Sri Michael Owens), with the help of these great ones, can accomplish.

Taking each new participant through the levels of transformation to prepare them for the acceptance of a new way life in The Way of Truth with the Light and Sound has required at the request of Dan Rin that the Sehaji step forward and guide the new consciousness of these souls along this path of unfoldment.

Why it Doesn't Concern The Way of Truth if the Participants Have Strong Affiliations with Other Paths of Life

The Way of Truth is the new storehouse of the higher frequencies of the Light and Sound and all the other ways of life that have this essence within them. By the orders of the great Oversouls of this universe, The Way of Truth has been focused to fill the hearts of those not yet awakened to their true purpose of being. If they have sought through other ways of life to touch the Heart of God, The Way of Truth can only sharpen the perceptions of the seeker. The Way of Truth brings light and love and does not withhold anything from the heart of the seeker who wishes to be with Sugmad.

Why God is Called Sugmad in The Way of Truth and the Role Sugmad Plays in Its Mission on Earth

The name of God has often been used to describe existence and is sometimes believed to not truly carry a complete meaning for the power that it yields. Sugmad, an ancient term, embodies in Its vibration the true essence of beingness in all realms. It contains within Itself all aspects of being, positive and negative, and holds them in complete balance, to allow the true essence of the Light and Sound to permeate all of existence. The vibration holds the true sense of the power of love in this and all universes and in itself is timeless. The vibration of Sugmad touches in every being that sense of soul, Its true vehicle of love and experience.

How Many Were Led as Soul to Find Out More about The Way of Truth

At this time in the evolution of this Sugmad, it is necessary to bring into the consciousness of all beings the idea of the true self. You have been awakened by the Light and Sound and are seeking to understand your true self. Beyond the Physical, Astral, Causal, Mental and Etheric Planes lies the true essence of being, soul. With the change in the frequency of the Light and Sound, that which sends God's love throughout this universe has touched you in this place of existence, the soul, and like the magnetic pull of a collapsed star, you are moving toward the awakening of your true self in Sugmad. The Way of Truth was designed to carry soul to the state beyond Self-Realization to the center of beingness in the realms of the God Worlds or God-Realization, being one with the essence of love found in the heart of Sugmad. All life vibrates to the Light and Sound and beyond life is the eternal existence of soul. The Way of Truth was created to provide a door for the knowledge of the Higher Realms of existence to be shared in this physical existence in the lower bodies as we make the pilgrimage back to the Heart of God. It is the doorway to the God Worlds and is given by the Great Ones in the hierarchies of the spiritual realms for all to experience in this lifetime if you so choose. It is not by chance that you have been brought to this doorway, because the need for open-hearted souls to further the expanse of Sugmad's love is of much importance in today's world.

Why Soul Wants a Connection with Sugmad through the Light and Sound

Master Rumi:

Love is the true expression of soul through the Sacred Heart in all realms above and below the Great Divide between the Worlds of Illusion and the Great Sea of Love and Mercy, where souls exist in the Heart of God as one with that love. Sugmad presents Itself to us through the Light and Sound, which is what carries the infinite love of God to all beings in this and all realms of existence, inside and outside of this galaxy. The Light and Sound can be felt with the purest of hearts on the Inner Planes of existence when it is tuned by the love song to God, the HU. This sound purifies souls as they journey so that they may enter into the Higher Realms of the God Worlds to share in the magnificent wonders of Sugmad's love. We have brought to you The Way of Truth as a path to this new joy found in the Light and Sound because Sugmad wants all to share in the love that binds this universe together. Once you have seen your true self as soul through the teachings of the Sehaji Masters and the support of the Living Master of the Light and Sound, the desire for this connection to Sugmad can be fully realized through the Light and Sound. You shall be blessed by this grace and held in the infinite arms of Sugmad.

The Awakening

The feeling of your true essence will come to you.
Those who walked before this way will come to you.
All existence is focused through you,
For the love of Sugmad is timeless in you.

~ Rumi ~

How Reincarnation Relates to Soul's Connection to the Light and Sound: Knowledge

When Spirit is reborn into the manifest after its rest in Sugmad in the cycle of reincarnation, the lessons of karma that design its next journey are kept in the karmic scroll by the Lords of Karma. For soul to progress along the path of its enlightenment, reference to past life activity is of much benefit as soul searches for Self-Realization. In The Way of Truth, the path to God-Realization, the karmic balance can be changed, if necessary, through a connection to the Light and Sound. As soul comes to realize that it can walk in the God Worlds, aware of its existence in the Heart of Sugmad, it is sometimes needed to adjust certain karmic duties that may restrict the growth towards God Consciousness. The Light and Sound carry the knowledge from the scrolls of karma and can be accessed when soul steps on to the path toward Godhood. The tuning of soul's ability to journey to the temples that house the scrolls is a process of the Light and Sound being infused into soul's involvement in sharing the love of Sugmad. Through the HU and a sacred word given by the Living Master at the time of initiation, soul is offered the chance to reevaluate its karmic past and perhaps be granted a change when it begins to love through an open, selfless heart of God Consciousness. The vibration of the Light and Sound carries soul through its growth and learning and is the companion that will lend itself to answers to the questions that may perplex new initiates as they move through the many levels of awareness in the journey to higher consciousness and then to complete God-Realization in The Way of Truth.

The Goal for All Souls to Attain in This Lifetime: the Shared Love of God

In your true self, as part of the great love of Sugmad, soul is the identity that at some point you see reflected in all your experiences in the Lower Realms of Beingness, the Worlds of Illusion and Duality. As in many lifetimes before, you now have the opportunity to evolve far beyond your wildest expectations if you choose to grow toward the awareness of Sugmad with your being; that is to say, to become a God-Realized soul. As you begin your study in the Mystery School of The Way of Truth, the evidence of this part of being becomes exceedingly clear with each initiation toward a greater consciousness of the love that is a part of your true being. It's when this is awakened in your human consciousness that you at last sense what life truly holds for all who open themselves to the love of Sugmad.

Why The Way of Truth is a Path to God-Realization

The Way of Truth was specifically designed by the Sehaji at the request of Sugmad, the Grand Council and the Silent Ones to provide for those of true selflessness a way to expand the joy of love in this universe. This path has been tested in other forms of the teachings of the Light and Sound, and now its purity of heart has been accomplished through the efforts of Dan Rin, the Living Master of the Light and Sound, to clarify the waters of the spiritual seas. This is offered to those who have seen in themselves a need to be in touch with a greater purpose of love and caring in their lives. The call to this teaching also touches those who have felt stagnation in other forms of spiritual teachings where the presence of the Light and Sound has been diminished by the egos of those seeking self-approval at the expense of other spiritual seekers of truth. The Way of Truth has brought back into this universe the fire of the selfless heart for those who are destined for mastership in the God Worlds through the guidance of the Sehaji Order of Masters and the Living Master, Dan Rin. The path to God-Realization is the foundation of the search for participants in The Way of Truth. God-Realization prepares the initiate for the duties of the

Godman when he or she has come through the karmic cycles presented for his or her growth through many lifetimes. To step once again on the familiar planes of consciousness of the Higher Realms is the reward for the long journey you have taken in this lifetime. You are welcome to this path if you so choose to experience your true self once again in soul.

A step by step exercise with a mantra for the participant to use to make a direct connection with the Light and Sound

This exercise is intended to give the participant their first initiation when they use it. At this point if you have felt the touch of the Light and Sound and heard an Inner voice saying it is now your time, there is a simple step to take to begin to realize your true purpose in being and to start on a path that will revitalize your heart to the love that has been yours through time immemorial. This exercise is given by the Living Master of the Light and Sound, Dan Rin, as a way to open the door of your Sacred Heart so that it can be filled with the desire of contact with that which will move you into a state of wonderment and begin to walk the path before you in The Way of Truth.

1. Sit in contemplation using the Third Eye (the center of the temple between your eyebrows in the middle of your forehead) to focus on the heart within the center of your being.

2. Let your breathing be slow and steady.

3. The word "HU" has been mentioned before as a way to allow you to feel the love of Sugmad. Chant this word softly five times.

4. Then ask within your heart that the Living Master of the Light and Sound, Dan Rin, be present with you as you look into yourself to feel the love of Sugmad for the first time entering into your true being, that of Soul.

5. As you sit with your eyes closed, imagine a vibrant, gold light surrounding you. This is the presence of Dan Rin gently lifting you out of the illusion of the world of duality to show you for the first time in your heart the essence of your true self in Soul. Hold this feeling as long as you can.

6. After the contemplation, take pen and paper and, without thinking too much, write about your experience. Share this with no one. Repeat this exercise for one week. You will feel your heart begin to open and may sense your first connection to the Light and Sound. This will be the beginning of your journey in The Way of Truth.

Blessed Be.   ~ Sri Michael

~ Level Two ~

From Contemplation to Universal Soul Movement

Explaining Contemplation and the Practicing Steps of its Use

Master Milarepa

We are all students of Sugmad's love and contentment, and, even in the use of the tremendous love that is at hand, this study will demand a methodology of understanding its use and needs in daily life on all planes of existence. The path to this understanding is availed by seeking within on the Inner Planes of awareness the guiding message that has been placed for your discovery. Sitting quietly with focus on your Third Eye and feeling through your heart with eyes closed will open a new and wonderful communication with a part of your being that should just be coming into focus as a part of your awareness. From this place, the Light and Sound can begin to enter and add to your experiences in the Inner world and life that has been opening to you. To facilitate this experience, you may use the word "HU" as a mantra to bring greater intensity to your first efforts to contact the Inner worlds of awareness. You also may have been given a sacred word to use to help you to be in contact with the Living Sehaji Master on the Inner to bring you along this new path. Take what you find in this place and let your heart hear it and then write whatever may come to you about the experience. This is called contemplation. Unlike meditation, it allows for interaction with the energy that comes through the heart via the Light and Sound. This communication will give some answers and will offer some guidance from the Inner spiritual masters who step forward to aid in your journey toward the Heart of Sugmad. This is a place where the Living Sehaji Master, Dan Rin, will speak to you and answer questions of the heart's expectations. From this place, he will guide you to other Inner masters who will bring a new presence to the wisdom that is already within you on how to progress as you seek new levels of awareness in all Realms of Beingness. Trust in what Dan Rin brings to you in these times of contemplation and use the guidance offered to you during this long and wonderful journey you have chosen to take in The Way of Truth.

Why the Contemplative Exercises Are Recommended to be Done Daily

Master Kusulu

This Inner world that has just been opened to you is vast and wonderful, but must be traveled with the help of the Living Sehaji Master, Dan Rin, for in your journey here you will encounter things that will be of great force and new to your consciousness. The daily practice of contemplation is like any other process of learning, and, if practiced well, it will result in great benefits. As Dan Rin shows to you the methods to reach the place of knowledge necessary for your unfoldment, he will leave you with instructions on how to return to these Temples of Wisdom and archives of knowledge. Through the daily practice of contemplation, you shall receive much of the training that is being offered to you on this path to God-

Realization. As you are new to this process of awakening, it is necessary to revisit these temples to gain from the knowledge that can be placed in your consciousness there. If you wish to be filled with the wonders of the Inner Realms, the practice of daily contemplation will strengthen your ability to bring more of your experience to the lower levels of consciousness from which you operate in your daily life.

The wisdom for your journey to your true self as soul is of great benefit to all that may come into your path as you grow toward the God Worlds. Do not look to understand these things with the mind, for they are specifically tuned to be communicated through the heart. As you gain merit in your journeys, you will be given an understanding of your soul mission in this Outer life in the Worlds of Illusion and Duality governed by Kal Niranjan, who oversees your karmic path as you progress on this road of awakenings. There are other levels of awareness that precede the steps into Soul Consciousness, which is placed from where even greater comprehension of the God power begins to enter into your being through the Light and Sound. The call to the Higher Realms of Being will start to gain strength in you and the presence of Sugmad's love will draw you closer to your true purpose of being in that love.

Understanding Universal Soul Movement and its Practices

Master Tremulen

As a student in The Way of Truth, a path to God-Realization, you will pass through realms of consciousness as you approach your true self in soul. The Astral, Causal, Mental and Etheric Planes are passed through as your initiations take you closer to the love of Sugmad. Each of these realms carries its own characteristics in awareness in the Inner journey that you will experience, and at each one you will gain valuable lessons on the Inner Planes as well as the Outer (or physical) Planes to strengthen you for the steps into the God Worlds. There are other universes that can be seen and other types of life that will be encountered as you travel these realms above the Etheric Plane. The vehicle that is given to you is your true self as soul to examine these wonders and to learn more of all aspects of being in the Heart of Sugmad's love. Once you have stepped into this level of beingness, that of soul, the transition to gaining more understanding takes on a new methodology, that of Universal Soul Movement (USM.).

Universal Soul Movement, unlike the idea of Astral Travel that you may have experienced in lower levels of consciousness, is not connected to the response felt in the Causal Plane, which is how the Astral adventures are shared within the Lower Worlds. Universal Soul Movement offers the ability to retrieve information from beings of other realms and to transport that information back to this realm where it is translated into useful information, for the vastness of Sugmad's knowledge goes far beyond the confines of this universe as we know it as soul and reaches into many other aspects of being.

Moving toward God-Realization requires a complete change of the vibratory structure of your being to receive complete access to the full benefits of the Light and Sound as the conduit of Sugmad's love to all that exists in this moment. The vehicle of soul can carry within its heart the information necessary to change the karmic balance laid out by your Soul Contract. It prepares you for the great mission of soul as it rises to the God Consciousness level and assumes its karmic duties in the changing karma of this time in this Sugmad. What is needed of you is to continue in your contemplation practices to gain the abilities necessary to understand the vast awareness that will be needed as you travel the Inner Realms moving toward your Godhood.

The Relationship between Contemplation and Universal Soul Movement

In contemplation comes the direction from the Living Master of the Light and Sound, Dan Rin, as to the purpose of your call to this way of life in The Way of Truth. The participants of this way of life have a very precise and well-defined mission - to bring the great love of Sugmad to all souls that have been denied the warmth of Its immense power in their lives. The initiations that come are directed via the Inner awareness of the Living Master from the Great Ones that prepare you as soul for your place in the Higher Realms of Beingness. It is through contemplation that the necessary changes are made to karmic duties, the sensitivity to the new frequency of the Light and Sound and the ability to understand the knowledge that is being passed from entities of other origins than this universe, which sometimes are encountered during Universal Soul Movement.

The information needed to maintain the correct frequencies in the vortices that feed the healing energy to the Light and Sound anchored in certain places in this universe and on this planet has to be maintained as part of the karmic duties of the participants of The Way of Truth. Dan Rin has gone through extensive training to be able to manipulate the Light and Sound and is the one who has brought it to the peak of efficiency in this temporal reality for the initiates to use in their duties here. During contemplation the student is trained by the Master to be of maximum use to this Sugmad.

How Universal Soul Movement Expands the Spiritual Consciousness of the Practitioner

Master Kadmon

The rate of transformation in the souls of this universe has been put in a very delicate balance and is supported by the energy brought from other parts of this universe. As the awareness of soul grows in the participants of The Way of Truth, each of you has the responsibility in your Universal Soul Movement to bring certain information to the Living Master as he is guiding you through the karmic duties in the time of change and growth. In order to be the vessel of knowledge that is being sent to this universe, the practice of Universal Soul Movement is essential to maintain the flow of the Light and Sound. As your heart begins to sense its true, selfless nature as soul, the vibration of the love of Sugmad that pours through your consciousness is raised to higher levels. It begins to prepare you for your travels in the God Worlds as you move toward mastership in the Great Sea of Love and Mercy. In times to come, you as soul will navigate this plane of existence as the captains of your own destiny in your usefulness to the love of Sugmad to many other beings. In the form of Spirit, soul is the greatest messenger of love to other beings that will be encountered as the mission of this Sugmad is fulfilled. You shall, in your own growth, see what the true meaning of the transparent, selfless heart carries to those that wait in other Realms of Beingness, as The Way of Truth is destined to bring the message of Sugmad's love to them.

How Universal Soul Movement Brings a Joy of Living and an Appreciation of All Life to the Heart of the Participant

In the awareness of the soul's process of unfoldment in this time through Universal Soul Movement, the selfless heart sees and feels the presence of Sugmad's love in all transactions in the universe. Traveling these Realms with the assistance of the Living Master affords the participant of The Way of Truth to return with the spark of the Higher Realms to which it has journeyed. As all things are changed by interaction with the Light and Sound, so it is when soul touches the fabric of eternal existence during its journey to the infinite Realms of Beingness. When the selflessness of the Sacred Heart is touched, it translates into great joy and is transmitted to all other realms of existence, including those in the Lower Worlds of day-to-day living. How this is felt completely by the participant is in the heart exchange that takes place with all that come within the aura of the student. As the participant is drawn closer to the God Worlds during Universal Soul Movement, the intensity of the Light and Sound bathes the traveler with the purest love of Sugmad, leaving with them the overwhelming sense of well-being that is felt when held in the arms of Sugmad's love for all.

How Universal Soul Movement Facilitates a Connection with the Light and Sound Leading all the Way to the Heart of God

Master Rumi

Love is the ultimate fuel that charges the soul in its journeys to other Realms and brings it closer to its selfless Godhood in the Higher Realms. The pure love of the transparent heart is the highest frequency exchange of the Light and Sound that can be experienced in the form of communication with the Lower Realms. As you lift your hearts to be touched by Sugmad, the Light and Sound sends through the opening of the heart a direct message from the center of beingness that It is present and is transmitting the highest frequency of love to the soul who is seeking the true, selfless connection to the Light and Sound. The Master can see and will grant passage to those who seek only to bring this great love into existence in the hearts of all beings and to be charged with the duty of transformation of the Light and Sound into accessible frequencies in the realms below the Great Divide to guide souls that have not felt the complete warmth of Sugmad's presence in this universe. This love is that which draws every being in existence back to the Heart of Sugmad.

Why Participants use a Mantra during Contemplation and throughout their Day

Master Rebazar Tarzs

Any rhythmic and harmonic pulse that can cause in the heart a desire to be closer to the Light and Sound can be called a mantra. The use of such a word or sound is the doorway in your contemplation that allows soul to be released from the present situation that the Lower Bodies may be engaged in so that it may move unencumbered through the Higher Realms of being. In your morning contemplation, you seek to understand what is to be a part of your mission each day to spread the love of Sugmad and to bring it forward in your consciousness to be used during the course of the day. The use of "HU"or your sacred word spoken Inwardly will bring the vibration to the encounter that you have been led to as part of your daily, karmic duty as a carrier of the Light and Sound in The Way of Truth and releases the love of Sugmad into the exchange taking place. This effect is carried to all Realms and brings greater stability to the infusion of the Light and Sound in this universe and to this planet as this great healing of the karmic past takes place through the city of Ekere Tere.

A Universal Soul Movement Exercise

1. Sit quietly and bring the focus of the Third Eye to the Sacred Heart, the center of being within your Inner self.

2. Sing *"HU"* five times and call for Dan Rin to come to your aid by saying his name five times slowly.

3. Make the request that you would like a better understanding of the art of Universal Soul Movement.

4. Open your heart to sense your true existence as soul and offer it to him to carry.

5. Very slowly say, *"HU - NAT - SUM"*(HÜ NÄT S∂M) five times.

6. Each time, you will feel a slight sense of acceleration as if taking off in a sphere of light.

7. In your experience, know that the Living Master is with you and is guiding you through this brief excursion into Universal Soul Movement and that you will feel the change in your involvement with the Light and Sound at the conclusion.

Blessed Be.

~ Level Three ~

The Protection of the Inner Master

Why The Way of Truth has a Living Teacher who is an Inner Master and an Outer Master

Master Tremulen

As a student in this mystery school of The Way of Truth, guidance in your unfoldment comes from the Living Master of the Light and Sound, Sri Michael Owens, also known on the Inner Planes of God as Dan Rin. In these two capacities, he is available to you to help direct you in your journey at all times. There are many questions about and explanations for the changes that you will be experiencing, and as you share these with the Master on the Outer in the form of Initiate's letters [also called reports], it will give Sri Michael the chance to respond to you and offer you guidance on the Outer.

When in contemplation, it is often suggested that you call on Dan Rin for help in spiritual matters that may not translate into words for you but just unusual feelings. In the form of the Inner Master, he will be better able to show the necessary steps to resolve what is happening with you in your unfoldment process. To seek this communication with the Master in both these Realms is of great importance to assure a strong growth in your quest for God-Realization. Know that personal exchange with the Master is difficult because of the simple limitation we experience in our physical forms, but is well balanced with the availability on the Inner.

How the Two Aspects of an Inner Teacher and an Outer Teacher Render Love and Protection to the Participants of The Way of Truth

Because the realms of the Inner world contain many things that are not of a nature that you may understand and could bring some harm to you as you venture into this area of being, the presence of the Master on the Inner is vital to your protection. His great love for you in the Outer realms will be felt in areas of your life at unexpected times or at times of confusion or doubt. Sri Michael as the Living Master has been charged with this duty to all the participants in The Way of Truth, as you are of great importance, and Sugmad truly loves all of you, for It has given you Dan Rin.

How the Practice of Universal Soul Movement Connects the Participant with the Schools of Higher Learning called Wisdom Temples in the Inner Worlds

The awareness of your true self as Soul has been activated in you and you feel the need to let this consciousness grow within you. As Dan Rin guides you on the Inner to the places of great wisdom in your Universal Soul Movements, he will at this time give you protection from unseen forces that may wish to misdirect you along the path. Universal Soul Movement is the best method of accessing these places. As they exist only in the Inner Realms of consciousness, and, as you are new to this, the request of Dan Rin's presence is always necessary for safe passage through these planes of consciousness that are new to you in your Soul Awareness. From these places, you will receive knowledge on the Inner that will show itself to you when it is needed on the Inner and the Outer Realms of existence.

How the Inner Master Works with the Participant during Universal Soul Movement and in the Dream State

The Master can place in your consciousness in the dream state certain tasks to test your desire for this journey that you are taking. All participants must seek through the Sacred Heart this way of life that will make them one with the love of Sugmad. There can also be vital information as to how to respond to adversity that you may encounter while in Universal Soul Movement with the Master so that you can respond quickly in times of sudden change on the Inner. All that appears is not as it truly is, and the protection and direction of the Master must be listened to and followed at all costs, and so some directions are imparted to you in the dream state and stored in your Inner consciousness for use at later times during Universal Soul Movement with the Master.

How the Inner Master Introduces the Participant to Other Past Teachers of the Light and Sound

While working with you on the Inner, the Master can bring into your awareness the ability to recognize Souls who have been masters and have reincarnated to assist in your development on the Outer. These past teachers of the Light and Sound have been placed here as part of their Soul Contract to assist Dan Rin in your training for your possible mastership. Lessons will not be announced, but you will be advised when you have passed through an experience that was for the benefit of your growth in the Light and Sound. In your Inner journeys with the Master, he will at times bring you into the presence of other teachers of the Light and Sound who have been assigned to help prepare you for some part of your Soul Contract which is being formed as you grow in awareness of soul.

The Meaning of "Sehaji" and Identifying Some Masters of this Order

Milati, Rebazar Tarzs and Agnotti - three of the Sehaji Order

Sehaji is the vibratory description given to the masters of the Inner Realms who are of great wisdom and provide guidance for the students of the Light and Sound who show great merit and desire to live in the God Consciousness of selfless love and devotion to Sugmad. They serve from the middle path, the path of non-power, the true God power that shapes the destiny of souls who travel the Inner Realms moving towards the God Worlds. They are far beyond any of the spiritual teachers who have passed through this temporal existence. Their lineage cannot be traced, for they have always been present in the soul of Sugmad and will always be a part of the fabric of Its love.

How the Sehaji Work with the Living Sehaji Master, The Way of Truth and its Participants

As Dan Rin brings each of you along this path of growth toward your true self and toward mastership in your own right, the Sehaji are enlisted to give aid when certain areas of Soul Contracts or karma are uncovered and may need specific attention from a master of special merits. Each has the ability to change the direction of soul's growth if there is need for it. The balance of Sugmad is forever changing. Based upon the contingencies of Free Will in this universe, the Sehaji awareness governs all restructuring that needs to take place to afford the greatest results in Sugmad.

Opening the Heart to Universal Soul Movement and Making Contact with the Sehaji Masters

To prepare the heart for the journey within, the participant must become familiar with the path they will be following, assisted by the Master Dan Rin. The consciousness of the Sacred Heart must be laid open to receive the riches of

Universal Soul Movement and the teachings of the Sehaji Masters on the Inner Realms.

Master Rebazar Tarzs

We of the Sehaji Order wish to accept you in these Inner worlds of learning, but one must come with an open heart to gain the understanding of the ancient secrets and wisdom that has been chronicled for eons.

1. To prepare for this journey, sit quietly and focus your mind on the Third Eye in the center of your forehead.

2. Then let your consciousness move to the center of the heart charka and sing the "*HU*" five times slowly.

3. Call to Dan Rin three times very slowly, asking him to help you open your heart to the Light and Sound that will guide you to us.

4. To let your self move to your beingness in soul, use the word "*SU TALAY*" (SÜ TÄ LÄ). This will generate the vibration to allow you to move with Dan Rin into a deeper experience of Universal Soul Movement and to be introduced to the many Temples of Wisdom and knowingness that,

as you gain a deeper awareness of your true selfless heart, entrance will be granted to you.

Blessed Be!

~ Sri Michael

~ Glossary ~

A

Astral Plane The Astral Plane, also called the Emotional Plane, is the powerhouse for physical movement. A more sensitive transformer of the higher energies than the Physical Body, this plane is also the realm of the emotions.

B

Best-Laid Plans Sugmad's dream for its creation of the universe and all life forms; a dream in which sleeping souls tested, tried and proven through the fires of purification eventually awaken. Once fully awake, Sugmad's children see each other as brothers and sisters, person to person, nation to nation. Love, peace, harmony, and Sugmad's abundance reign.

C

Causal Plane The Causal Plane was created as a storehouse for memory to be accessible for the use of soul in any of the Lower Worlds.

Charity Charity is a gift of love with no strings attached.

Contemplation This is an active form of engaging the mind in activity aligned with soul, and in this way, differs from prayer and meditation.

D

Darshan Darshan **is** a gift of love from the Godman that fills the recipient's heart with joy, for the face of a living God has been seen.

E

Ego A part of the mind, ego's purpose is survival. Too often seduced by power, in actuality, the ego is like a ping pong ball when compared to the sun.

Etheric Plane The Etheric Plane, sitting just below the Soul Plane, is the highest region of the Mental Plane, and was created to begin soul's descent into the Lower Worlds.

F

Forgiveness Is one of the keys to ascension and spiritual achievement. To truly forgive, one's soul must be filled with compassion.

G

God-Absorption Involves seeing, knowing and being a son or daughter of Sugmad. It is the ultimate reunification with Sugmad such that when you move, Sugmad moves.

God-Realization The cellular recognition, ignited from within, that you are a part of God.

Great Divide This refers to the separation of the heavenly worlds from the Lower Worlds. Below the Great Divide points to the worlds below the Soul Plane; above the Great Divide considers planes inclusive of the Soul Plane and higher.

H

Heart Center The Heart Center is located around the physical heart, however the term refers to this area as a chakra or a location that acts as a conduit for divine energy.

HU HU is the sacred gift from this Sugmad to the souls of this universe who are ready to receive the heart of its truth. As the final key to the highest plane in the long journey through all the Lower Realms of this universe back to the

Heart of God, it can open every door. Use HU to seek the destination of your heart.

I

Initiations Initiations acknowledge souls passing tests on their journeys home to the Heart of Sugmad. They provide structure and catapult souls to new uncharted territory in each successive plane of their journeys.

Inner Inner describes the focus on that which is not seen with physical eyes, but exists as experiential phenomena nonetheless.

J (none)

K

Kal Niranjan Kal Niranjan was designated by Sugmad as Lord of the Lower Planes. Kal is not malicious or vicious as he has been portrayed. He merely carries out his assigned duties with precision and deft artistry.

Karma Also known as the Law of Cause and Effect, karma is the law by which soul reaps the rewards or experiences of the consequences of prior actions, even from past lives, whether soul remembers them or not.

L

Law of Compassion This Law allows soul a way to give love under any circumstances.

Law of Freedom Freedom creates, contains, and maintains the vital energies of life. This Law enables Sugmad to learn of Its true and full potential.

Law of Noninterference This Law renders respect to all life. This is accord with Sugmad's gift of Free Will to all souls, and allows souls to evolve in their own unique ways.

Law of Silence Little understood, but greatly needed, silence is pregnant with power. Silence holds great energetic *frequencies of the Light and Sound.*

Law of Unity This Law is a reminder that our true goal and state is union with Sugmad and one another.

Life Contract A Life Contract specifies a mission; it gives direction as an agreement to move in certain areas to gain awareness and expertise unique to self in relation to others to fulfill a greater purpose.

Light and Sound These are the primary emanations from Sugmad that constitute the Life Force, source of all life and All That Is.

Love Love is the essential nature of Sugmad, soul, and all manifestation. Love creates and sustains our universe; the absence of love destroys.

M

Mental Plane The Mental Realm, or mind without physical brain stuff, was made to take the intuitive impulses and step them down a few notches more. The Mental Plane includes the Etheric, however, the Etheric is of a higher vibratory quality and sits directly below the Soul Plane.

N

Non-power The non-power is the receiver, the receptacle of Sugmad's Power. To experience the non-power, one must achieve true detachment with full loving awareness.

O

Outer Refers to phenomena that can be perceived by the physical senses, as distinct from "Inner."

P

Physical Plane The Physical Plane was created for souls to experience gross and corporeal beauty and pain through sensory apparatus. As the lowest plane, it completes Sugmad's playground and grand experiment for the education and evolution of souls, sparks of Sugmad's own Self, units of Sugmad's awareness.

Q *(none)*

R (none)

S

Self-Realization This is the first stage of soul's entrance into the heavenly worlds as it journeys into these worlds of beingness and pure love. Here the aspirant recognizes her or himself as Soul, not as the Lower Bodies soul uses to gain experiences in the Lower Worlds.

Soul Soul is a part of God, "made in His image" and is actually the same in nature as Sugmad.

Soul Contract In each incarnation, soul enters with an aim or a purpose. As reductive units of God, we each have unfolding to do based on the karma we have created. A Soul Contract is an intelligent agreement that directs a particular soul's growth toward its ultimate destination, reunification with God.

Soul Movement/Universal Soul Movement Soul movement or Universal Soul Movement is a change in consciousness through which soul perceives realities beyond those that exist in this Physical Realm. Some may experience a movement in their Soul Body as it travels through the various dimensions; others may simply become aware of a phenomenal experience without any sensation of movement.

Sugmad This constitutes a pure name for God, the Creator of this universe and all life forms.

T

Third Eye (Also called Middle Eye) Located a little above the space between the eyebrows and about an inch within, the Third Eye is a receptor of Inner visions. The pineal gland is its physical representation. The Middle Eye is a doorway that soul opens to begin its Universal Soul Movement into the worlds beyond the physical veil. It opens the spiritual connection between the practitioner and a greater flow of Spirit.

Temples of Wisdom These are Inner temples where spiritual training, purification and the imparting of secrets occur. These spiritual temples are contained within vortices of varying degrees that transmit frequencies coming from the highest realms.

U

Universal Laws Sugmad established universal laws to bring order into consciousness from chaos. Like a train track for trains, or the Internet for ideas, universal laws provide a structure for creation and manifestation.

V *(none)*

W

Worlds

The *Higher Worlds* refer to creation starting from and extending beyond the Soul Plane up to the fountainhead of Sugmad or the Sea of Love and Mercy.

The *Lower Worlds* encompass creation just below the Soul Plane, specifically the Etheric Plane and down to this, the Physical Plane. The gap between these two sets of worlds is called the "Great Divide."

X *(none)*

Y *(none)*

Z *(none)*

~ Index ~

A

Abundance, 27, 200, 204, 142, 152, 189, 306

African
    Renaissance, 4, 10, 25, 28, 59, 85, 102, 111, 205

Agam Des, 9, 108, 119, 236, 242, 248

Agnotti, 20-21, 91, 119, 302

AH-LA-HU, 141

A-LA-TU-SEN-TA , 158

AH-SWAY-LO, 147

Allah, 128, 131

Alexander, Archangel

Althea, Archangel

Angelic Orders, 90-92, 117, 215

Angels, 28, 52, 61, 94, 108, 119, 219, 259 (See also Althea, Alexander, Gabriel, Mary and Michael)

Appreciation, 30, 102, 126, 163, 190, 243

Brahm, 48, 57

Bridges of Peace, 10

Brigit of the Picts, 114

Brotherhood of the Sehaji
Masters of the Celestial
Seas, 74

Buddha, 9, 85, 117

C

Cameroon, 13

Career, 18, 164

Causal Plane, ***

Challenge, 79, 171, 173,
195, 200, 240

Charities, 90

Child of God, 39

Children of Light, 43, 118

China, 246

Choices, 62, 79, 93, 101-
104, 130, 164, 188, 244

Christian Apostolic
Community, 113

Circles
    Eighth, 36, 48, 54, 114,
237
    Fifth, 94
    Seventh, 6, 111, 235,
237
    Twelfth, 36

City of Ahirit, 87

City of Pure Light, 9, 116,
205, 213

Code of Three, 67

Commitment, 11, 36, 50,
52, 159, 163, 207, 239, 267

Compassion, 70-71, 85,
134, 160, 162

Communication, 28, 65, 87,
286, 294

Confidence, 63-64, 106,
173, 223

Connection, 18, 32, 140,
143, 147, 156, 159, 277, 279

Energies
  God-Realized, 28, 37

Engrams
  Family, 86
  Fear, 46
  Latent, 48
  Negative, 47, 54, 89,
120, 154, 212
  New, 50

Essenes, 82

Etheric
  Body, 26, 37, 59, 131

Evolution, 21-22, 41, 110,
119, 124, 225, 274, 276

Egypt, 13, 115, 155

F

Facsimiles, 59, 83

Faith
  Blind, 6

Famines, 85, 221

Father of All, 118, 227

Fear
  Residual, 59, 154

Fifth Plane, 35, 88, 92, 223

Freedom, 14, 47, 57, 137

Free
  Will, 30, 32, 34-35, 79,
87, 91, 99, 138, 157, 205,
212, 246-247, 303

Flower, 23, 167, 185, 214,
223, 245

Focus, 18, 43-44, 62-67, 76,
79, 103, 140, 143, 150, 158,
165, 170, 174, 200-201, 205,
207-208, 240, 246, 251-252,
283, 286, 296, 304

Friendships, 105-106

Fubbi Quantz, 84

G

Gabriel, Archangel, 9, 34,
36, 80-81, 91-92, 117, 120-
121, 127, 130-131, 161-162,
167, 215-217, 248, 252-253,
259

L

Labyrinth, 39, 173

Lai Tsi, 7, 20

Lavender Order, 48, 83, 85

Law
  Of Assumption, 61
  Of Compassion, 160,
310
  Of Forgiveness, 135
  Of Freedom, 137-138,
310
  Of HU, 152, 186
  Of Karma, 153, 309
  Of Love, 124, 159, 186
  Of Neutrality, 47, 120
  Of Non-interference,
310
  Of Non-power, 47
  Of Opposites, 211
  Of the Planes, 54
  Of Silence, 80, 82, 114,
136, 161, 180, 188, 198, 207-
208
  Of Soul, 153
  Of Threes, 39-40, 46
  Of Unity, 211-212

Lazarus, 82, 248

Lemlet, 99, 110

Lemuria, 24-25, 66, 115,
215, 221

Leytor, 38, 53-55, 58, 109,
139

Life
  Contracts, 77

Light
  and Sound4, 6-10, 14-
15, 17, 20, 24-25, 27-29, 36,
39-40, 42-44, 49-50, 52, 56-
57, 65, 67, 71-72, 74-77, 82-
84., 94, 100- 101, 104, 108-
109, 111, 115, 118-119, 131,
134-1135, 139, 141-143, 145-
146, 153-154, 161-163, 175,
191, 193, 198, 210-212, 217-
218, 222, 235-237, 240-241,
246, 254, 263, 268-284, 286-
287, 289-297, 299, 301-302,
304, 310
  Giver, 14

Literature, 217, 227, 240

Living Sehaji Master, 3, 10,
14, 72, 74, 77, 86, 143, 208,
237, 286-287, 303

Lords of Karma, 12, 88, 279

U

V

W

10148384R00225

Made in the USA
Charleston, SC
11 November 2011